It's *Not* *Your* Money

Finding the Peace of Putting God First

Shelby ▮▮▮

Blessings!

Be Courageous

Be Intentional.

It's *Not Your* Money

Finding the Peace of Putting God First

JOSEPH B. GALLOWAY

DEDICATIONS

To Mary, the Mother of our Lord,
who told me, while I was visiting
the Basilica of St. Mary in Minneapolis,
to take *It's Not Your Money* national.

To Mr. John Smith, my high school
algebra teacher, who taught me
the truest of Financial Planning principles.

TABLE OF CONTENTS

It's Not Your Money

MEMORARE

Remember, O most gracious Virgin Mary, that never was it known that anyone who fled to your protection, implored your help, or sought your intercession was left unaided. Inspired with this confidence, I fly unto you, O Virgin of virgins, my Mother. To you I come, before you I stand, sinful and sorrowful. O Mother of the Word Incarnate, despise not my petitions, but in your mercy, hear and answer me. Amen.

"God has not given us a system of commerce, or roads, or an economic (or political) system. The gifts God has lavished upon us are far superior to any of that.

God gives us everything we have. Everything we own comes from God, including the gift of life. And what does God want from us? To be just as generous towards others."

Bishop Kenneth E. Untener

FOREWORD

They say that Grace comes in two forms: 1) a shutter-click glimpse, or 2) a long persistent, never-failing, always-on drip feed. Either way, God is banking on our getting it somehow or other. Can God bank on you? After all, it's not your money, your life, or your will that brings meaning to a human life. It is the will, the way, the truth of God that brings life.

When I shared with Joe what was to become the first of many spirited conversations about giving, I could see in his eyes a quest for fidelity to God. I could also see the legal mind he has, the love of things pragmatic, and the joy that comes from the Roman Catholic Church's rational layout of a still yet mystical God.

From-through-to. This sacramental principle leads. First things first. It's not yours.

FROM. Everything comes from! Unless you can count the leaves on the trees, the grains of sand on the seashore, or the stars in the sky, unless you can tell your mom how you were made—when even she cannot while it was happening in her—then you must attribute things to a giver—God. He is the Creator and Sustainer of all things.

THROUGH. This glorious God shares His blessed life with us, making us in His image and giving us divine possibility. God gives/creates, and we can also! God forgives a debt, and we can also! And so, you see the movement of God, which is designed by God, happens if we allow it. If we seek Him, know Him, love Him, we must give. Thank God He chooses to give you life, and even greater HIS life within you—the Holy Spirit.

Lastly, TO. While God seems as if He cares about everything—and why wouldn't He if He made everything?—there does seem to be a preferential option for the poor, the falsely thought second class, those cheated or excluded. Ever read Matthew 5:1-12? It's a list of God's special people—the hurt, the mourning, the simple, the peacemakers. These people, like those in Matthew 25:31-46 are the "TO." All of this is to please the Lord. These people are His concern, and so they become ours. They are the "to" we are to attend to as we try to please the Lord.

What Joe is trying to share is that God is Awesome! God is not asking for much when He asks for 10 percent of our time, talents and treasure. You keep 90%!!!!! But make sure you get the relationship right. The whole thing, this life, is a gift. Stewardship then, is simply saying thank you, Lord; we understand where this comes from. Thank you for allowing us to have any measure of participation at all. May we give you all the Glory in what we produce and in what we return to you.

Fr. Patrick E. Tuttle, OFM
Greenville, South Carolina
May 2020

Finding the Peace of Putting God First

Take courage, be stouthearted!

Psalm 27: 14

INTRODUCTION

It's Not Your Money

That's a bold, in-your-face statement right out of the gate. How often do I hear a prideful, bowed-up response, "What do you mean it's not my money? You are out of your mind. I worked for it. I earned it. I deserve it."

No question that we work and earn. But consider, just for a moment, where your abilities and opportunities to earn come from. In Deuteronomy 8: 10-18, Moses tells us,

"Remember to bless the Lord for all the benefits He gives. Do not forget the Lord. For when you have eaten your fill, and increased your gold and silver, and built your fine houses, you become haughty of heart and forget the Lord. You say to yourself, 'It is my own power and the strength of my own hand that has obtained this wealth for me.' Remember, it is the Lord your God who gives you power to acquire wealth."

This passage really hit home for me when my kids were little. We'd go to McDonald's from time to time. I'd bring their Happy Meals to the table, spread out the burger wrapping, dump the fries out, and grab a few for myself. They'd swat at my hand and howl, "Keep your hands off my fries."

I corrected, "Your fries? How did you get those fries? I gave you your fries. You wouldn't have any fries if I didn't get them for you." Then it hit me. What about my money? How do I get my money? Where do my talents, interests, and abilities come from that allow me to earn my money? Hmmm...

Here's another impactful verse: (1 Chron 29:11-12,14)

"Yours, Lord, are greatness and might, majesty, victory, and splendor. For all in heaven and on earth are yours...Riches and glory are from you...everything is from you, and what we give is what we have from you."

So, yes, you sweat and toil and earn money by God's grace and gifts to you. Still, you worry about money. Almost everyone worries about money. Money worries cause stress, anxiety, anger, and fear. It is a major cause of divorce. At the root of all this fear is a lack of faith.

This book will challenge your thinking and strengthen your faith by teaching what God says about money and possessions. In fact, God has a lot to say about money. Did you know there are over 2500 Bible verses that reference money and possessions? More than any other topic. God knows how pervasive money is to the everyday economy of our lives. Can you go a single day without spending money? Even if you didn't open your wallet or purse to pull out cash or a debit card, you probably took a hot shower. You probably drove your car and ate a meal. All of that requires money. Shouldn't we be interested in what God says about something as ubiquitous in our lives as money?

In this book we will compare and contrast what God says about money with society's best advice for what should drive decisions about money and possessions. You can probably guess that God wants us to be generous and trusting. Surveys show we Catholics have room for improvement. A study published by Notre Dame's Institute for Church Life found that Roman Catholics, as compared to other religious groups, are exceptionally modest givers. It found that only 15 percent of Catholics report giving at least 10 percent of their income, compared to over 27 percent of the rest of the church-going population doing so. Additionally, the study found that two-fifths, fully 40 percent, of Catholics do not donate to any cause, including the Church.[1]

Villanova's Center for Church Management finds that Catholics are the second lowest-giving Christian denomination, and that the average weekly gift to the collection plate is $10.[2] That makes me wonder if we Catholics think of going to Mass and putting money in the collection basket as competing with other ways we may spend our entertainment time. I imagine the thinking going something like this: "I pay a little over $10 to go to a movie. Mass isn't as entertaining, but it's Mass. So, $10 seems about right."

This book is about finding peace by putting God in charge. We seem to have a huge disconnect between money and our spiritual life, but our spiritual life often has more to do with our checkbook than with our prayer book. It's as if we tell God, "Lord, you are first in every facet of my life...except for money. Don't worry about that part of my life, Lord. I can handle that on my own." My personal and professional experience tells me differently.

The utmost goal is *metanoia*—a profound change of heart. It's about going deep in our relationship with Jesus, trusting and doing what He says. Remember the challenge Jesus gave to Peter in Luke Chapter 5 at the very beginning of His ministry? Jesus had just called Peter to follow Him. After preaching to the crowd on the shore, He told Peter to put out his boat into deep water for a catch. Even though Peter had been unsuccessful after fishing all night, he obediently trusted Jesus and did what He said. And the result was a catch so large that it tore the nets! That is what trusting and obeying Jesus does for us. The results are surprising and life-changing.

Trusting God and changing our attitudes about money changes our hearts, changes our lives, changes our families, changes our world. In these pages, you will find nuggets of information that will challenge your current thinking about money in good ways, ideas that will give you pause to think about what is most important in your life, and guidance that will serve to bring you and your family closer to Christ. By embracing the message of this book, you will find a sense of peace about money and financial planning that surpasses worldly understanding.

Who am I to be telling you all this? First, I am a lay person, a widower and father, soon to be remarried. Like most of you, I grapple with the money and spending issues that most of us face. I struggle with wanting more and spending beyond the edge of my income. I worry about saving for education and retirement and handling the intergenerational squeeze of helping children and supporting elderly parents. I puzzle over how these demands will impact my lifestyle choices. And I wonder how in the world I can fit giving into an already tight budget.

I worked for 35 years as a Financial Planner and Investment Advisor. Raised Protestant, I've always been interested in knowing the Bible. In an effort to infuse my work-life with my faith, I began a financial stewardship ministry called It's Not Your Money™. My story is one of God's nudging me to go deeper in faith, trusting Him to be courageous with my giving, and how that changed everything. I hope it will inspire you to courageous generosity. Please keep reading.

Do not conform yourselves to this age
but be transformed by the renewal of your mind,
that you may discern what is the will of God,
what is good and pleasing and perfect.

Romans 12: 2

CHAPTER ONE

Speak Lord, Your Servant is Listening

My Stewardship Story

I confess I have not always trusted God, at least not with the mundane, everyday stuff. It was easy for me to defer to God's omnipotence in the big issues of life, but I decided that I'd take care of the rest. I subscribed to the quote attributed to St. Ignatius, "Pray as if everything depended on God; act as if everything depended on you." So, act I did. I wanted to be in control, especially when it came to everyday decisions about how to spend money. I didn't need help making money decisions. Truthfully, I didn't want to submit those choices to God, lest He tell me "no."

In my work as a financial planning and investment professional, I analyzed budgets, planned savings goals and objectives, and developed investment strategies for hundreds of clients. I lived and breathed financial markets as if I were personally responsible for every down day of the stock market and every interest rate change and the resulting impacts on accounts. I was immersed in those topics for my clients and my family. By many measures, I was successful. That success led me to be engrossed in the proverbial keeping-up-with-the-Joneses syndrome, concerned for what others thought about the clothes I wore, the car I drove, and the house I lived in. They had to be good enough, but not too expensive.

Otherwise, it might give clients an opportunity to question if my fees were too high. I wore Jos. A Banks suits, not Brooks Brothers. I drove an Infiniti, not a Mercedes. How silly.

The point is that worrying about appearances caused spending that pushed the very fringes of our budget. I'd get frustrated at myself at month's end because the amount due was often more than the available balance of our checking account. I'd stress about how to make more money. Of course, I could have adjusted our spending, but that might impact the image of success I was trying to portray. It might mean having to turn down entertainment invitations, or change some aspect of my public persona that others might notice. They might think less of me. I might have to admit personal shortcomings, and maybe lose some control—as if I ever had any control. That led to more worrying. A vicious cycle. A merry-go-round. Somebody, please, help me get off!

We rocked along the traditional path of pursuing the American dream according to what we read in *Money Magazine* and *Southern Living*. Everything was fine, as it should be. Or so it seemed. From the curb, we looked like the All-American Family. But inside, we were frazzled by the time demands of three young kids' activity schedules on top of worrying about money all the time. No big deal. All our friends were in the same situation.

Even so, something gnawed at me. What was it? We were doing what we were supposed to be doing financially: I had the right amount of life insurance and contributed to the 401k, at least enough to get the full company match. We didn't skimp on Christmas presents. We went on nice vacations. But something was amiss. Honestly, I knew what it was, but I didn't want to admit the truth. Our spending was too frivolous. And we weren't giving as we should.

Let me share a little more of my personal background. I grew up in New Orleans where my family went to a Presbyterian church. I attended a Christian high school that was owned and run by a Baptist preacher and his family. I later taught and coached there. I credit the Baptist expression of faith as having the greatest influence on me. I learned life lessons there that carry me through to this day. As related to money, I understood that Baptists focus on tithing. That was what stewardship was all about. Stewardship meant tithing 10 percent of income. Period. Expected. An obligation.

Being from south Louisiana where virtually everyone is Catholic, I met a Catholic girl in college and married her. When our children were born, it became important to us that we worship together as a family. After visiting various churches, I signed up for RCIA and was confirmed as a Catholic in my late twenties. I then learned the Catholic definition of stewardship. It is much more comprehensive than just giving money. It is about how we live our lives. In a word, Stewardship is Discipleship. We acknowledge that God provides everything. He is the source of all we are and all we have. And in grateful response for all His many blessings, we are to give back of our Time, Talent, and Treasure.

This was a wonderful and exciting revelation to me. No more pharisaical laws to give 10 percent—or else—preached with pounding fist from the pulpit. Though I couldn't quote chapter and verse, I knew a lot of Bible passages on tithing from my Baptist days. But as Jonah tried to hide from God, I hid from those scriptures. In my experience attending Mass, stewardship was only rarely the subject of the homily so it was easy to hide. When stewardship was preached, the emphasis seemed to be more on time, on volunteering to help in various ministries. At least by comparison to my Baptist experience, the money part of giving was ignored, or at best, down-played. It sounded something like TIME, TALENT, (and, oh yes, sshhh – ah… treasure).

This was fine with me because my budget was already strained to the max, like a button on a fat man's shirt just about to pop off. I'd get frustrated because I'd want to buy a new tennis racquet. I wanted my late wife to shop for any clothes or household décor she wanted. I wanted my kids to have the latest video games and the newest gadgets. And of course, we'd all need the newest iteration of smart phone. These added expenses weren't in the budget, but I'd spend the money anyway and get the stuff. And at the end of the month—negative. Heaven help us if the A/C went out or a car would need major repair. I'd think, if only I could make a little more money. I'd ask, "Why Lord? Why aren't things going the way I want them to? I'm honest. I have integrity. I go to Mass."

In truth, I knew why. I wasn't tithing.

At Mass when the collection plate was passed, I'd put in some of the cash in my pocket. Sometimes, I'd even put all of the cash in my pocket. But I never carried much cash. I knew we should be giving more, but I couldn't figure out how giving more fit into our budget. After all, we were a young family with three sets of braces to pay for and college tuitions to look forward to. I needed to save for my own retirement someday. And, oh yeah, I wanted a bigger house with all the modern updates, a golf weekend with the boys, a Caribbean vacation, a new…. You know how this goes.

Whenever my kids would complain, in response I'd drone on about how when I was their age, I'd have to walk barefoot to school, uphill both ways, in the snow. They caught on to that tall tale more quickly than I admitted the source of my financial distress. I wasn't doing what I knew God wanted me to do.

STEWARDSHIP REFLECTION

In 1 Thess 3:12, Paul begs that the Lord make us increase and abound in love for one another and for all. I love that—Lord, make me increase in love. Make me do the right thing.

How often do we avoid doing what we know we should do? We can pray, "Lord, make me do what is right. Make me love better. Make me listen intently. Make me speak gently. Make me be generous."

Lord, make me a good steward. I know everything comes from you, and I know I am to give back. I know it's not my money.

A business associate and I were talking about faith and money matters over lunch one day. He asked me, "What made you do it?" He wanted to know what caused me to become serious and intentional about giving. As I reflected on his question, I remembered the testimony of a friend who spoke at Mass on a Stewardship Sunday. He shared his and his wife's decision to give 10 percent, even though they didn't know how that would work in their budget. The numbers didn't add up. But, they were just going to do it. They were going to trust God and do it.

That was a gut punch for me. I knew I was to tithe, but I was scared what that might do to our spending. Would we have enough to do the activities we enjoyed and buy the things we needed? I was afraid we'd have to give up something—what? How painful would the adjustments to our spending be? Would my kids be deprived of anything? We didn't want them being made fun of at school because they didn't have the right brand of sneakers. Would we still be able to take vacations, or even go out on a date to a nice restaurant? We didn't know.

I was embarrassed by my concern. Things weren't going the way I'd planned. I worried too much about money. I couldn't go out and get whatever I wanted whenever I wanted it. Money was too tight. But why? I knew our budget was out of alignment with God's overarching plan for spending, but I could justify just about any expense. I wanted to be in control of spending decisions. I didn't want to cede that to God or anyone else. I didn't want to trust God to provide for our "needs," and I certainly didn't want anyone but me deciding what those "needs" were. What I really needed was a massive dose of courage. I needed to trust. I needed to move the Bible passages I knew from my head to my heart.

I needed the courage to have faith to trust God.

My friend's testimony had obviously hit a major nerve. On the way home from Mass that day I had this self-talk:

"I believe all I have is a gift from God."
Dt. 8:18
Remember, it is the Lord your God who gives you the power to acquire wealth.
1 Chr. 29:12 Riches and honor are from you, and you have dominion over all.

"I know I am to tithe."
Dt. 14:22
Each year you shall tithe all the produce you have sown.
CCC 1969
The New Law practices the acts of religion—almsgiving, prayer, and fasting.
CCC 2447
Among these (works of mercy), giving alms to the poor is one of the chief witnesses to charity. It is also a work of justice pleasing to God.

"I understand tithing means 10 percent."

Gn. 14:19-20

Abram gave one-tenth of everything.

HCBD

A tenth part of one's yearly income set aside for sacramental purposes.

"I am to give of my best."

Nm. 18:29

From all the gifts you receive, and from the best part, you are to consecrate to the Lord your own full contribution.

"Which is from my first fruits."

Prv. 3:9

Honor the Lord with your wealth, with the first fruits of all your produce.

Dt. 18:4

You shall give him the first fruits of your grain, and wine, and oil.

"And I am to do so cheerfully."

2 Cor. 9: 7

Each must do as already determined, without sadness or compulsion, for God loves a cheerful giver.

"I am convicted. I will do it."
"If I ignore this, I rob God."

Mal. 3: 8-10

Dare a man rob God, but you are robbing me…in tithes and offerings…bring the whole tithe into the storehouse.

"And worse, I sin."

Jas. 4:7

So for one who knows the right thing to do and does not do it, it is a sin.

"But, I will trust God."

Jer. 17:7-8

Blessed are those who trust in the Lord…They are like a tree planted beside the waters…they do not fear heat when it comes.

Ps. 128:1-2
Happy are those who fear the Lord, who walk in the ways of God.
Mt. 10:28-31
Do not be afraid...Are not two sparrows sold for a small coin? Yet not one of them falls to the ground without your Father's knowledge...You are worth more than many sparrows.

"He has provided; He will provide!"
Mt. 7:8-11
For everyone who asks, receives; one who seeks, finds; and the one who knocks, the door will be opened...How much more will your heavenly Father give good things to those who ask Him.
Heb. 13:5
Let your life be free from the love of money, but be content with what you have, for He has said, "I will never forsake you or abandon you."
Prv. 11:24
One person is lavish, yet grows still richer; another is too sparing, yet is the poorer.

"By God's grace, I will do it."
Jos. 24:15
Decide today whom you will serve...as for me and my household, we will serve the Lord.

An ongoing discussion with my late wife commenced that afternoon. It was more a one-sided tirade directed at myself. The litany of questions went something like this, "Where's the money for vacation going to come from?" "What about saving for our children's college educations?" "How will you feel when we have to decline a double date to dinner and a play downtown?" She took this for about a week, patiently absorbing my rants like a down pillow receives a tired head. Finally, after Thursday's dinner and another agitated round of monotonous questions, she looked at me with soft eyes and asked, "What are you afraid of?"

Bug-eyed incredulous, with jaw dropped to the table, I said (to myself), *Huh? What? I ain't afraid a nuthin.*

She continued, "Just do it. I trust you, and I trust God will provide for us. He always has."

BAM! There it was. Another gut punch. I wish I could report that our giving went up cold turkey that next Sunday to the full ten-percent tithe. In reality, it was more of a giving progression. The next step was a decision to be intentional about our giving. Instead of haphazardly giving some or all of whatever cash I had in my pocket, I started writing a check. Twenty dollars. Most weeks. $20 per week adds up to $1000 for the year, a decent amount. It felt good to give, and after doing that for a while, I noticed I didn't really feel it.

The next step in the progression was to fill the gap. Writing checks made our giving more, but if we missed Mass or were out of town, we didn't give. So, I became even more intentional and signed up for online giving. That way, no matter what, my parish could count on my support. And while I was at it, I raised our offering to $25 per week, $100 a month. I felt good about all of this. I felt that I was beginning to do what I was supposed to do.

Another big step came about 15 years ago. A sermon challenged me by asking if I was giving an amount that corresponded to the blessings in my life. I remember getting all huffy in the pew, thinking, *How dare him. I already give a lot. I mean I give to United Way. I give to the Bishop's Annual Appeal. I give to all kinds of things. And I have to help support my in-laws. On top of that, I give $25 per week to this church. I wonder how many others give that much* (as if it's a competition).

But as my prideful annoyance faded a bit, and I thought more about the homily, I began to count my blessings. I had to admit that even when all-totaled, the decent sum we were now giving to church and charities still didn't add to 10 percent of income. Sure, we made some sacrifices—we ate out less—but we didn't feel that we were really missing out on anything. The message of the homily began to sink in. Maybe I should increase our offering. I felt the urge to increase our giving to $40 per week.

Now that gave me pause. The old fears crept in. $15 more per week? Could I afford it? My oldest was in college with two kids behind him. I should be saving more for retirement. We had already cut back on some lifestyle expenses, but could we cut more? I didn't really want to. And I didn't want to have to sharpen the pencil to scrutinize my budget any further. But did I trust God to provide—or not? I gathered up my courage, stepped out in faith, and increased our weekly giving. And what happened? I gained a sense of peace that I cannot explain. It was terrifying. But it was liberating. We experienced a release, a feeling of freedom.

Deciding to do what we believed God wanted us to do, instead of falling back on our fears, gave us a sense of peace and a joy that does not make worldly sense. But, the peace born from obedience to God's Word, as Paul says to the Philippians, is beyond our understanding. That was the "a-ha!" experience for me. That was when we decided to put God first in every area of our life, including our finances. We created a new spending plan with tithing as the first expense. Sure, we had to cut back on some recreational expenses, wah, wah. But so what. We now had confidence it was the right thing to do. This new spending plan never caused an argument or resulted in disappointment. In fact, whenever we felt a twinge of aggravation or remorse due to missing out on some fun, we'd remember the reason why cash flow was no longer available for that category of expense. We would relax and our hearts would soften, welling up in a feeling of joy. It's a paradox. Giving and thus giving up what we once thought brought us happiness, now brought an even greater sense of joy. That's the *metanoia*—the profound change of heart and renewal of mind. What a tremendous blessing!

When we decided to put God first in our budget, our attitude toward money and spending shifted. Every spending decision became a stewardship decision. That large latte with a shot of espresso I got every morning on my way to work added up to $70 a month! I started pouring my own coffee into a travel mug and began putting that $70 into the collection plate. We used to spend $150 per month for cable TV service to have access to 150 channels we didn't watch. I now pay about $25 per month for 10 channels, half of which I still hardly ever watch. That freed up more money for giving. Going out to for dinner versus cooking at home. Buying a burger for lunch versus bringing a sandwich. You get the idea.

Don't misunderstand, it hasn't always been sunshine and roses. We had our share of struggles, but who hasn't? One internal battle I fought was whether I was using my talents in the right way. Here I was working in an industry laser-focused on money and worldly wealth. I enjoyed serving people in an important area of their lives. I enjoyed the challenge of trying to understand the markets. God gave those interests and desires to me. I thought that put me in a position to counsel people on godly attitudes toward money. But was that more a rationalization, an excuse to assuage any guilt I might have about constantly focusing on helping people and myself accumulate more money and acquire more stuff? Honestly, I was attracted by the income potential of the job. Sometimes I'd rationalize that I should try to make as much money as possible so that I could give more of it away. Other times I wondered if I should do something different, something that I perceived had a greater impact on people.

As I was often told when expressing this conflict to friends and family, I needed to get over myself. The Bible does not elevate any one job over another. God doesn't care if you are a teacher, a doctor, a janitor, a cashier, or a financial advisor. Paul's letter to the Colossians teaches us that what God cares about is that in all that you do, you do as if for Him (Col. 3:23). What God cares about is that you utilize the talents He gives you to the best of your ability to serve Him and build His kingdom.

Those internal background struggles burst to the forefront with the 2008 – 2009 market crash. My income dropped to a third of what it was before. As Job said, "The Lord giveth and the Lord taketh away. Blessed be the Lord" (Job 1:21). Like almost everyone, we had to make tough choices. But we continued to tithe. In fact, I remember a business partner asking me if I was still giving in the midst of the crunch. I told him I was. I admitted the amount was less to be sure because my income was lower. But that's okay. As Paul tells us in 2 Cor. 8:12-13, "If the eagerness is there, it is acceptable according to what one has, not according to what one does not have, not that others should have relief while you are burdened." And you know what? We never missed a meal.

We also experienced serious medical challenges and the accompanying expenses. My late wife fought cancer for fourteen years before she was called in from the battlefield. Got it at 43. Treated it. Beat it. Then it came back. Five more times. And while she is now completely healed in heaven and at peace, there was a lot of physical and emotional strain over the years. She could justifiably have harbored anger toward God for allowing periods of severe debilitation while trying to raise school-aged children. But she never blamed God. She never questioned, Why me? She would even tell you that she was blessed. She would not let cancer steal her or any of our joy.

That attitude toward her illness was a testimony to her strong faith. It was a tremendous witness to me and others and allowed me to hold steady in my own faith. The way our family and friends and our church community surrounded us through the ordeal was awe-inspiring and overwhelming. Humbling. Like her, I never felt anger toward God for putting us in this situation. I never considered withdrawing from church or withholding financial support. Those responses seemed to me to be akin to an "I'll show you—I'll hurt me" kind of response.

The grieving since has, at times, been draining. But again, even in the middle of all that junk, I have been and continue to be tremendously blessed. And in those blessings, by the grace of God, I am grateful to make returns of even more time and treasure to the Lord.

After my first wife died, my financial planning issues turned to questions of legacy. What important life lessons do I want to live beyond me? How will my estate plan communicate God's priority in my life? I'll address these questions in more depth later in the book.

So why write this? Is it to get you to tithe more money to the church? Sure, the church needs money to operate, but it's not about the church's getting your money. It is about your giving, though. It is about your *willingness* to give, your trust in God, and the *attitude of detachment* from money and possessions. Giving is vital to our spiritual well-being. It is one of the best expressions of gratitude we can make to God for all the blessings He gives us. Giving money demonstrates a mature discipleship and makes a strong statement of faith and trust that God will provide.

Ask yourself, "What has power over you?" Whatever it is, it could be the root of idolatry. Turn it over to God. Trust Him with it. Otherwise, it may be keeping you separate from God. If you worry about money, obviously it has power over you. Turn it over. Do you cling tightly to things, to images of success? Then these have power over you. Turn them over. Let them go. C. S. Lewis once wrote, "A person whose hands are full of parcels cannot receive a gift." Turn them loose. Lay those burdens down.

Not worrying does not mean not caring. Nor does it mean acting imprudently or haphazardly. Instead, not worrying about money is a huge step toward a trusting relationship with God. How we handle money directly reflects the intimacy of our relationship with God. Do we believe Him? Do we trust Him?

Do you think of money and finance as a spiritual component of your life? Shouldn't you? Think about it, can you go a single day without spending money? You may not use cash or a debit card. But certainly, you used resources that cost money. Shouldn't something so pervasive in the everyday economy of our lives be an integral part of what should be our most important relationship?

Read on to learn not only what the Bible says and the Church teaches about money but also how to make those lessons come alive in your life. How to make it happen! When I started tithing and trusting God with my finances, money worries melted away. It changed our lives. Inform your faith and decide for yourself. Trust God with your finances. It will change your life.

Speak Lord, Your Servant is Listening

"You can give without loving,
but you can never love without giving."

Victor Hugo

CHAPTER TWO

I believe; Help My Unbelief

Why Live a Stewardship Life?

Thank you for turning the page. I hope you can see something of yourself in my story. What about your story? What do you want in life? What do we all want? I remember early in my career always wanting to make more money. I often thought, Man, if I could just make $5,000 more, then I could.... But once we get past the material and get serious, most likely what we really want, at our core, is to be happy and content, to have less stress. We think that money will gain those benefits for us. Maybe it will for a short time. Now let's go deeper. Stop for a moment and reflect on your answers to these questions: Who are you? Who do you wish to be? For what are you striving?

Fair warning: this is deep stuff. Tedious. Difficult. Think of this chapter as playing three dozen scales before performing for the recital. It'll be like pre-season training, two-a-day practices in the smothering August heat and humidity before the start of football season. This will be the grueling early morning calisthenics in dew-covered grass, and the hot afternoon's focus on fundamentals. But you know you can't win the State Championship without getting through August. So, lace up your cleats, snap your chin strap, and let's go to work.

Ideal

Most people have a life philosophy, a set of core beliefs that informs who they are and guides how they act. Think about your personal life philosophy for a minute. What drives you to be who you are?

- What is most important to you?

- What are you enthusiastic/passionate about?

- What is the meaning and purpose of your life?

- What/Who inspires you?

- What are your goals and objectives?

- What motivates you to action to achieve these? Why?

I had the privilege to attend a Christian high school where I learned lessons about the meaning and purpose of life that I rely on to this day. One was that God made me and knows me personally. The creator of the universe created me and wants to be in relationship with me. Another is that He loves me unconditionally. Out of love, He gives each of us unique talents and abilities. Our job is to discover and develop these to the best of our ability and use them to serve God. I believed that, then and now, but I'm not sure I fully understood as a young adult how I was to apply that principle to my life in a practical way. I had vague notions of doing my best, having a successful career, and providing for my family as measures of employing the talents God gave me. So, I set out to achieve those ends in the typical worldly ways.

Many people cite a spirit of rugged individualism, instilled at our founding as the Land of Opportunity, as the primary motivator of their actions. We think that it is of our own abilities that we learn and cultivate skills, that we create opportunities, and that we are solely responsible for the results. We achieve success and enjoy comfortable affluence, thinking we did it on our own in our own way. Author and Leadership Consultant Ken Blanchard calls these folks "Driven People." He writes,

"Driven people think they own everything. They own their relationships, they own their possessions, and they own their positions. Called people are very different. They believe everything is on loan—their relationships, possessions, and positions."[3]

In truth, God is the one who gives each of us the ability to learn and work. He gives us our particular likes and dislikes. We order our priorities accordingly. Philippians 2:13 says that "God is the one who, for His good purpose, works in you both to desire and to work." Thus, you develop the ideas that you like—your aspirations. You then direct your actions toward accomplishing those ideas that rank with the highest priority. These high-priority aspirations are what give meaning to your life. In other words, they are your IDEAL.

How do you know what your IDEAL is? Consider these questions:

- What do you think about most?

- How do you spend your time—especially free time?

- On what do you spend your money?

Answers to these questions will give you a strong sense of your priorities, your aspirations, your Ideal. Ideals evolve over time. What is important to us and what motivated us in high school is different by college graduation and evolves even more in our 30s, 40s, etc. In high school, my Ideals were centered on girls and sports. In college, girls and sports, and graduation and a job. Now—girls and sports! Just kidding (hopefully). Shouldn't they be loftier?

The highest Ideal we can have is a deep, personal relationship with Jesus Christ. By our baptism, we are members of God's family and are called to glorify and honor Him and enjoy Him forever. How do we glorify God? How can we be better disciples of Jesus? By spending time developing our relationship with Him in prayer, attending Mass, studying the Bible, and being in community with and serving others. We glorify God when we courageously put Him first in every area and facet of our life.

Let's make those three questions a little tougher, just like fingering B-flat minor scales or running three extra wind sprints. Consider the following:

- How does your use of time and how you spend your money reflect the priority God has in your life?
- If reviewing your checkbook, would an outside observer find evidence that Jesus is first in every facet of your life, including money?
- Would Jesus see Himself in you? Would He see evidence of a generous spirit? Would Jesus see Himself in you? Would He see evidence of a generous spirit?

Pope Francis released an apostolic exhortation entitled *Gaudete et Exsultate*, subtitled "The Call to Holiness in Today's World." In it he explains that holiness is the mission of every Christian.[4] Holiness is discerning and doing God's will in our lives. Bishop Robert Barron, in his book *Letter to a Suffering Church*, insists that if we want holier priests and a holier church, we must hold ourselves to the same standards.[5] Each of us is called to Christian holiness. St. John Paul II said, "The ways to holiness are many according to the vocation of each individual."[6]

Pope Francis goes on to say that we need to see the entirety of our lives as a mission. That to walk the path of holiness requires prayer and contemplation alongside action. Action is charity lived to the fullest.[7] The activities of holiness are the works of mercy found in Mt. 25:31-46: feeding the hungry, sheltering the homeless, clothing the naked, welcoming the stranger, caring for the sick, and visiting the imprisoned. This passage insists that we are answerable for how we manage our material resources. These actions certainly require time, and often money. God is looking for us to glorify Him in the ways we use our time and capital in service to the most vulnerable neighbors among us.

When discerning our priorities and how our Ideals motivate our actions, shouldn't we strive, as Jesus says in Mt. 5:48 to be "perfect as our heavenly Father is perfect."? 1 Peter 1:16 says it this way: "You shall be holy, for I am holy." Being holy is not the same as being sinless. That is impossible. Even the apostles had their share of sinfulness—a crooked tax-collector, an impetuous fisherman, a zealot. Yet, we know them to be holy. Their holiness can only be attributed to its being a gift of God. Holiness does not depend on our merit, personality, effort, or achievement. It is entirely God's action and gift to us.

We need only to accept it.

We need to be aware of the moments of encounter where opportunities to do good confront us. Of course, we need help with this. I know I do. I get so caught up in the activities and demands of daily life that I am often oblivious to the needs of others, especially those beyond my family. To get this help, I often pray for the wisdom to know and the courage to do. Our path to holiness is knowing and being attentive to the needs of others, taking action and doing the good we can do, giving alms, and praying all the while.

Our Ideal, then, should inspire everyday efforts toward kindness and generosity. By God's grace, we should act courageously, with desire for the good of our neighbors. And we should give alms which serve to facilitate others' doing good. In these actions we serve the common good of our community. Others see the good works which then inspires them to act, all of which glorifies our God in heaven (1 Pt. 2:12).

Lily, a friend at church, lives it this way:

"This is my church. I love this church. When I see someone in need, I give. I help. I don't worry about it. When I'm in need, others see this and they give and help. It's amazing how it works. It all just works. I just give and trust and I don't worry about it. God takes care of me."

Amen!

Stewardship

The Ideal is to strive to be like Jesus. To be holy. To be a good and ever-improving disciple of Christ. That is what stewardship is. Stewardship is a conversion journey of receiving God's love and returning love to Him. God loves, and so He gives. We see in Psalm 112 that God gives lavishly. He gives us Himself in His son. And Jesus loves us so much that

He gave his life for us. As disciples, as stewards, we strive to be like Jesus and love and give.

Stewardship is often thought of in terms of giving money, as tithing. But it is much more than that. Let's look at the full meaning of the term. *The Merriam Webster Dictionary* offers this definition of a steward: "One employed to manage domestic concerns."

In the Catholic Christian context, the U S Conference of Catholic Bishops defines stewardship thus:

"Stewardship is an expression of discipleship, with the power to change how we understand and live our lives. Disciples who practice good stewardship recognize God as the origin of life, the giver of freedom, and the source of all they have and are and will be. The generous sharing of resources, including money, is central to its practice. Helping the Church's mission with money, time, and personal resources of all kinds is a serious duty, a consequence of faith, and not an option for those who understand what membership in the Church involves."

"Who is a Christian Steward? One who receives God's gifts gratefully, cherishes and tends them in a responsible and accountable way, shares them in justice and love with others, and returns them with increase to the Lord."[8]

Stewardship is Discipleship. It is how we are to live our lives. We acknowledge that everything is a gift to us from God. When we honestly accept and internalize that truth, then we are sincerely overwhelmed by His generosity to us. We realize how blessed we are. When I contemplate this truth, I am in awe, speechless. I can't believe He would be so generous to me. I certainly don't deserve it. And that's the point. He loves us so much that He gives us everything. He gives each of us unique talents and abilities, interests and desires. All is gift. Every aspect and area of our life is gift. Every. Single. Thing. Everything!

We receive Spiritual gifts:
Faith, Hope, and Love.

We receive Temporal gifts:
Time.
Our Talents and Abilities.
Our Interests and Desires.
Our Hopes and Dreams.
The Jobs we have whereby we earn money when we employ these.
Promotions and Layoffs.
Achievements and Accomplishments.
Successes, Disappointments, and Failures.
Weaknesses and Struggles.
Challenges and Obstacles.
Material goods and resources.
Leisure and Recreation.
Joys and Sorrows.
Our Fears and Concerns.
Our Family, Friends and Enemies.
Our senses—sight, smell, taste, hearing, feeling.
Our Health—at every stage.
Today.

Today is a gift. Right now is all we have. God is active in our lives today. There is no guarantee of tomorrow. So let us rejoice and be glad in today. How will we live it? Zacchaeus gives us a tremendous witness on how we are to live. When he encounters Jesus in Luke 19, he is overwhelmed by Jesus' love and acceptance, responding with great humility. When Jesus invites Himself to Zacchaeus's house, ready or not, he humbly accepts. When Jesus refers to him as a lost sinner, he is humble. And he humbly accepts salvation for himself and his house. In gratitude, he gives courageously: half of his wealth to the poor and a fourfold restitution to anyone he may have defrauded. His life is transformed. What a great example for us to follow.

When we embrace true stewardship, we can't help but respond in a positive way to Christ's call to live holy lives and glorify God. We shape our lives to imitate Christ. Stewardship becomes a mindset. We believe that all is from God and that we don't own anything. We are managers of what He gives us. We are to manage His gifts the way Jesus did. We are to live as Jesus did. How did Jesus live? He lived in total submission to God. How do we do that? First, we spend time with Him in prayer and contemplation. Then we live in, care about, and serve our various environments: home, work, church, the community at large. And in all humility, we recognize and admit that all we are and all we have are gifts from God.

When you stop to ponder your life and acknowledge God as the giver of all you have and are, how should you respond? If you know and trust by faith that God provides all your needs, then what do you think is asked of you in return? Mary models the truest, most beautiful response for us in her humble "yes" to God at the Annunciation in Luke, chapter one. Her obedience of faith is the standard God expects of us all.

FRUIT OF THE SPIRIT

HUMILITY
A socially acknowledged claim to neutrality in the competition of life[9]

Example: **MARY**
A teenage girl, acting on the truth she knew about God and herself, said "yes" to God. A model of what God expects of us; love God and leave everything else to Him.

James 4:10
Humble yourselves before the Lord and He will exalt you.

Proverbs 22:4
The result of humility and fear of the Lord is riches, honor, and life.

Luke 18:9-14
He who humbles himself will be exalted.

Obedience Leads To Freedom

Stewardship encompasses every facet of our lives, and so, of course, this includes our finances. How we live drives how we spend. We are to submit to God's authority over how we use our time, engage our talents, and spend our money. God is the master, the owner of all. We own nothing! Our role is to manage the gifts He allots to us to the best of our ability. And to do so for the benefit of our neighbors—His kingdom.

We all are stewards. The question is whether we are good stewards or bad stewards. We know we should be good stewards of all of our resources, including money. We should give more to the Church and worthy charities. We should volunteer more time teaching catechism, coaching kids, and serving in the food pantry. But life is busy and time is at a premium. We think in terms of scarcity. It is hard to give of what precious little spare time we may have. When it comes to giving money, we worry that we won't have enough to provide for ourselves and our families. We worry that we won't be able to spend at a level that makes us feel happy or successful or comfortable.

Feeling comfortable often means having more. Ours is a consumer society. Advertisers entice us to want what they deem is necessary for happiness. They tell us we will be more youthful and successful if we buy this or that product. No matter how many shirts and shoes we have, we want more. The three-year-old 65-inch flat screen will no longer do. We must get an 82-inch LED Smart 8K UHD TV. If we want to be Club Champion, then last year's PING G400 Driver must give way to this year's Callaway GBB Epic. We need to renovate the master bath and redecorate the living room. All of these things make us feel better about ourselves and our lives. All it takes is money, probably more than we have. Even if we have the money, do we truly need these things? More importantly, is this how the money should be spent?

Please read this next sentence slowly: How much of what we feel we need, what we think we should provide for our families, is instead just wants, truthfully nothing more than lifestyle choices?

Why do you work? Most of the clients I've served say they work to provide a "comfortable lifestyle" now and then hope to have a "comfortable retirement." What does that mean? For most, it means being able to maintain their current spending or even increase it a bit to allow for travel and luxuries. It means they don't want to worry if there will be enough money to last until they die. It certainly means not being dependent on children for support in their old age. A few will even admit a desire to become richer to enhance this level of comfort.

I think deep inside we all know that goals of this kind are not worthy of our Ideal. There appears to be little thought of God or concern for His Kingdom in the goal of a comfortable life. Though we may not mean it this way, working for a comfortable life has a selfish, inward focus.

Is it possible that instead, we might think of work as a mission field, as an outreach to those we work with and serve? Could we strive to bear the image of God to all who we encounter in our work environments? What can we do to think of work as more than just about making money?

Paul gave us a glimpse of how to do this when he was leaving the church at Ephesus. He reminded the presbyters, "In every way I have shown you that by hard work of that sort we must help the weak, and keep in mind the words of our Lord Jesus who Himself said, 'It is more blessed to give than to receive'" (Acts 20:35). So again, why are you working?

STEWARDSHIP REFLECTION

Why do we strive so fiercely for money? Psalm 49 tells us plainly that though we trust in our wealth, and with riches may count ourselves as happy, we can in no way redeem ourselves, and there is no price one can pay to God for life. Riches are transitory. We can't take it with us.

We are to strive for what has sustainable value—righteousness, love, patience, faith, gentleness, generosity, and endurance. If we truly believe that all we have is a gift from God, then whether from abundance or from lack, we admit that It's Not Our Money.

Work is important. We should seek to cultivate and employ our talents for the good of God's kingdom. Paul instructs the Thessalonians that if anyone is unwilling to work, neither should he eat (2 Thes. 3:10). God directs the work we do: "For God is the one who, for His good purpose, works in you to both desire and to work" (Phil. 2:13). Jesus says, "Do not work for food that perishes, but for the food that endures for eternal life" (John 6:3).

What I learned from my own effort to answer the question of why I work is that it is not about the kind of work we do, but why we do it. Why do we strive so? There is a proper striving, but it is not for more money or for a "comfortable retirement." Rather, it should be a striving after the Kingdom of God and trusting that He will provide all else to us besides (Luke 12:31). We should hold our dreams of career success and retirement loosely so that God has room to act in them.

That's what happened to me. I thought I'd work until 70ish and fade into the sunset. But by the grace of God, I heard a call to transition out of the financial advisory business and into financial stewardship ministry. I wasn't ready to retire. I hadn't accumulated enough money to meet my goal, or so I thought. But, do I trust Him, or not? So, by that same grace, I am trusting Him and trying to answer the call affirmatively.

Could it be that our rigid attachment to our own ideas about money and success is actually pride? Does pride motivate a sense of self-sufficiency and a desire for independence? Pride like this is a force that may make us believe that we are not dependent on God, but on our own abilities. That belief is actually spiritual warfare. Jesus told the rich man in Mark 10:21 to sell everything, give to the poor, and follow Him. But the man's pride in what he had and his unyielding ideas of what he could do with his money caused him to walk away. He was in a battle between what he thought his culture believed about success and what Jesus was telling him. We, too, battle with what the *world says* we need versus what *God says* we need. Think about it....

The World Says
There is no free lunch. You earned your money by your own efforts. You deserve it. It's yours. Do with it what you will.
God Says
Money, like all things, including the ability to earn it, are gifts from God. (Dt. 8:10–18)
The earth is the Lord's and all it holds (Ps. 24)
We are managers entrusted with using His gifts for the common good.

The World Says

To live a more fulfilling life, you need the right house, the right clothes, the right car to be happy. He who has the most toys, wins.

> **God Says**
>
> You brought nothing into the world, you shall not be able to take anything out of it (1 Tm. 6:8).
>
> Be on your guard against all kinds of greed, for one's life does not consist of one's possessions (Luke 12:15).

....

The World Says

Pay yourself first.

> **God Says**
>
> Tithe of the first fruits:
>
> Blessed be Abram by God most high…Then Abram gave Him a tenth of everything (Gn. 14:19-20).
>
> The choicest first fruits of your soil you shall bring to the house of the Lord (Ex. 34:26).
>
> The first fruits of your grain, your wine, your oil, as well as your shearing of your flock you shall give to Him (Dt. 18:4).
>
> Honor the Lord with your wealth, with the first fruits of all your produce (Prv. 3:9).

....

The World Says

You must have 20 times your salary saved in order to have a comfortable retirement.

> **God Says**
>
> There is no Scriptural basis for retirement from productive work.

....

The World Says

You need to make as much money as possible because success is measured by the size of my bank and brokerage accounts.

> **God Says**
>
> The love of money is the root of all kinds of evil (1 Tm. 6:10).

The World Says
If you give, you won't have enough for yourself.
> **God Says**
> Be detached, let go, give (Mt. 19:16-21)

....

The World Says
To be successful, you must do everything in your power, no matter what, no matter who you may hurt along the way.
> **God Says**
> Whoever wishes to be great among you will be your servant (Mark 10:43).

....

The World Says
If you only had _X_ dollars more, then you could get . . . then you could do . . . then you would find happiness.
> **God Says**
> Money is seductive and addictive and leads to idolatry, thinking that created things will bring you happiness.
> If you love money, you will never be satisfied. If you long to be rich, you will never get all you want (Ecc. 5:10-11).

....

The World Says
You must pursue riches, grasp for material rewards, and protect possessions. Life is a competition. You must look out for Number One.
> **God Says**
> Money and resources are to be shared in a neighborly way. The widow in Zarephath complained, "I have nothing baked, there is only a handful of flour left and a little oil, when we eat it we will die. But Elijah assured her, "Do not be afraid, for the Lord says the jar of flour will not go empty, nor the oil run dry" (1 Kings 17:9-16).

....

The World Says

You pay taxes; the government provides welfare. You don't need to give anything more.

God Says

Give to Caesar what belongs to Caesar and to God what belongs to God. (Mt. 22:21). The poor will always be with you.

Pay to all their due (Rm. 13:7).

True religion is this: caring for orphans, widows, and the poor (Jas. 1:27).

....

The World Says

After you've accumulated enough money, then give.

God Says

I shall store my grain, build bigger barns, and say to myself, "You have so many good things stored up, rest, eat, drink, be merry." But God said, "You fool, this night your life will be demanded of you" (Luke 12:16-21).

....

The World Says

"OK, I guess I'll give because I'm supposed to. Let me see what's in my wallet...."

God Says

For it is appropriate for you...to act willingly...for if the eagerness is there, it is acceptable according to what one has, not according to what one doesn't have (2 Cor. 8:10-12).

....

The Bible has a lot to say about money. Walter Brueggeman, in *Money and Possessions*, states that "the Bible is indeed about money and possessions and the way in which they are gifts of the creator God to be utilized in praise and obedience."[10] He contrasts our worldly economy with the economy of God. "Ours is an economy of extraction and accumulation. Fear lives here. Worry belongs to the practice of accumulation. We are stressed by the determination to build our bank accounts and acquire possessions, driven by a fear of scarcity, and a desire to conform to our society's idea of success. We feel we must hoard and protect our wealth from concentrated power which seeks to extract our wealth in order to transfer it to the more powerful."[11]

St. Francis of Assisi is credited with this quote: "It seems to me difficult and embarrassing to be possessed of worldly goods, which we can only preserve at a price of a thousand annoyances, often even being obliged to have recourse to arms to put a stop to the quarrels and lawsuits which arise there from."

Brueggeman goes on to say that Jesus offers an alternative economy, what He calls the Kingdom of God. God's gifts are unlimited and regenerative. His way is not the worldly way. It is not defined by supply and demand and scarcity. His capacity to bless us is boundless.[12] Jesus came so that we might have an abundant life (John 10:10). He will supply whatever we need in accord with his glorious riches (Phil. 4:19).

We know the stress caused by the drive to build our bank accounts. We know the worry about having enough. If we want to be rid of stress and worry about our finances, we must transform our attitudes toward money and possessions. Instead of striving to earn, spend, and accumulate, we should discern and conform to what God wants us to do with our money. Where can we learn about what God has to say? The Bible.

Consider these passages that support the sharing of our financial resources as the first priority of our spending:

Gn. 14:19-20
Blessed be Abram by God the Most High and blessed by God Most High who has delivered your enemies into your hand...And Abram gave Him one-tenth of everything.

Gn. 28:22
Of everything you give me, I will return a tenth part to you without fail.

Nm. 18:29
From all the gifts to you, you shall make every contribution due to the Lord, from the best parts, that is the part to be consecrated to the Lord.

Dt. 12:11
Then to the place which the Lord your God chooses as the dwelling place for His name, you shall bring all I command you: your burnt offerings and sacrifices, your tithes and personal contributions.

Dt. 14:22
Each year you shall tithe all the produce of your seed that grows in the field.

And our sharing is to be from our first fruits:
Ex. 34:26
The choicest first fruits of your soil you shall bring to the house of the Lord, your God.

Dt. 18:4
You shall also give Him the first fruits of your grain and wine and oil, as well as the first fruits of the shearing of your flock.

Dt. 26:2,10
You shall take some first fruits of the various products of the soil which you harvest from the land the Lord, your God, gives you... (Then you declare)... "Now therefore I have brought the first fruits of the products of the soil which you, Lord, have given me."

Prv. 3:9
Honor the Lord with your wealth, with the first fruits of all your produce.

And my favorite:
Mal. 3:8-10
You are robbing me. And you say, "How have we robbed you?" In tithes and contributions! Bring the whole tithe into the storehouse. Put me to the test, says the Lord of hosts. And see if I do not open the floodgates of Heaven for you, and pour down upon you blessing without measure.

Yes, I know all of these are Old Testament passages and that they sound so legalistic. But remember, Jesus Himself said He did not come to abolish the law, but to fulfill it: "Amen I say to you, until heaven and earth pass away, not the smallest letter or the smallest part of a letter will pass from the law" (Mt. 5:17-18). Even so, giving with the proper attitude is crucial. Listen to what Jesus tells the Pharisees in Mt. 23:23: "Woe to you Scribes and Pharisees—hypocrites. You tithe mint, dill, and cumin, and neglect the weightier matters of the law: justice, mercy, and faith." The letter of the law is not what's most important. The Scribes and Pharisees obeyed the letter of the law. Rather, it is the spirit of the law that we should embody. I think what Jesus wants is for us to be detached from material things, to see a need and respond generously, courageously, and intentionally, and without expecting anything back. We should not give out of fear, guilt, or obligation. Instead, we should give out of love and out of gratefulness for all of God's gifts and benefits. And we should give cheerfully (2 Cor. 9:7).

FRUIT OF THE SPIRIT

GENEROSITY

A fruit of the Spirit formed in us for eternal glory.
A virtue, a firm disposition to do good.[13]

Example: **THE DISCIPLES**
The disciples in Acts 11:27-30, who in response to the coming famine, determined that each, according to ability, would send relief to the brothers in Judea. In other words, in the face of a crisis, instead of hunkering down, they gave.

2 Cor. 8:2-5
(regarding the grace of God given to the churches in Macedonia)
In a severe test of affliction, the abundance of their joy and their profound poverty overflowed in a wealth of generosity on their part. For according to their means, and beyond their means spontaneously, they begged us insistently for the favor of taking part in the service to the holy ones.

The title of this section is Obedience Leads to Freedom. What do I mean by that? It is a paradox. We believe the Bible to be the inspired, inerrant word of God. We take it as authoritative truth, as directions for how we should live and act. As Brueggeman says, "The Bible is relentlessly material in its focus and concern. Everywhere, the Bible is preoccupied with bodily existence."[14] We commonly believe that to obey means to be hemmed in by rules, but freedom knows no boundaries. The paradox is that when we stay within the boundaries and obey, we get a feeling of peace, a release from stress, and a sense of freedom.

A high school friend told me of an event he attended where Kingdom Dog Ministries presented God's truths about obedience and how obedience leads to freedom. The trainer demonstrated how a trained dog strives to please its master and trusts that its master will provide. Envision a dog lying at the feet of its master on a front porch. It displays good temper. It is free to roam an unfenced area because it knows its boundaries. In contrast, an untrained dog must be inside a fence. You've probably seen how such a dog is on edge, agitated, barking. It is a paradox. The dog supposedly free to do as it pleases, free from the rigor and discipline of training, must be chained or fenced in and is actually less free than the trained dog.

So it is with us and our Master. Striving to truly please God with how we handle money, by giving and exercising discipline and restraint over our spending, frees us from worry and stress about finances.

The Bible is our training manual. Psalm 19:8-12 instructs us that the law of the Lord is perfect, His decrees are trustworthy, His precepts are right, His commands are clear, His statutes are true, and obeying them brings much reward. Saint Paul expressed well the paradox of knowing and not obeying in his letter to the Romans. He shared his struggle with why he didn't do the good he knew to do, but did the things he hated (Rom. 7:13-25). There is a rift between our desire for doing good and our actual performance. We can only be rescued from this conflict by the power of God's grace working though Jesus Christ.

God's grace gave me the faith to step out and begin tithing. The result was a relief from worry and stress over money. I experienced a warm feeling of well-being because I did what I believed God asks us to do with our money—which is truly His money. I gained a sense of freedom in resolving not to be controlled by desires or possessions.

God's grace strengthened my dear friend Ken at a very difficult time in his life. He honored me by asking for advice about how he should handle his new source of disability income from Social Security. He became eligible for that benefit at age 57 because his illness had advanced to the point where he was expected to die within the next year. We talked about account titles, beneficiary designations, and other end-of-life issues related to finances. As we discussed how his financial position would provide for his medical needs and the needs of his family, he decided to increase his to tithe to the church.

I was deeply touched, humbled. Honestly, I was surprised that he was even concerned about his giving in the face of his mortality.[15] Ken told me, "I wake up every morning and thank God for another day. I ask Him what He has for me this day. I am so blessed. He has been so good to me, the least I can do is give money to His church."

I was awestruck. Instead of anger over his medical condition and its refusal to be healed, Ken accepted his lot and still considered himself to be blessed. And in his blessings, he felt a need to give back. What a tremendous witness to all of us.

So, what is God asking of you, demanding even, in these Bible passages? Since this is a book on financial stewardship, let me ask you to think for a moment about the Treasure component of your life. How do you use your money? How much are you giving to the Church and other charities? Is it an amount that justly corresponds to God's blessings in your life? Now that you know what God is asking of you, what will you do with this? How do you feel when you don't do what you know you are supposed to do? Are you like Paul when he exclaimed, "Miserable one that I am," upon disclosing that he did not always do the good that he wanted to do. How might your life be better if you obeyed and acted on God's instructions? What are your obstacles to responding? At the very least, as Malachi challenges, shouldn't you test God in this?

STEWARDSHIP REFLECTION

Choose Life

Moses instructs the Israelites about their choice, life or death, in Deuteronomy 30. He exhorts them to choose life by following God's law. It is like that with your money.

You have choices on how you spend. How often do those choices result in stress and worry about whether there will be enough money at the end of the month? Instead, choose to follow God's laws about tithing.

Tithing is giving of your first fruits. It is choosing life. It just works. This doesn't mean tithing is all cookies, cake, and ice cream. There may be challenges in changing spending habits like there are challenges when giving up sugar. But both are good to do. So, choose to give and claim God's abundant gift of life. Tithe and rest in the knowledge that It's Not Your Money.

....

Our Response

The Parable of the Talents in the Gospel of Matthew provides a powerful example of how we should act in our role as stewards of God's gifts. The master gave three servants talents (literally, a measure of silver), each according to his ability. Two of them cultivated those gifts and returned them with increase to the master. You know what happened to the third servant. His unwillingness to act in faith and trust resulted in humiliation. As a result, what he had was taken from him (Mt. 25:14-30).

Everything we have is given to us like those talents given to the servants in the parable. God gives each of us unique abilities and interests, wisdom and knowledge, fortitude, understanding, and piety. Jesus chooses each of us to follow Him and bear fruit (John 15:16). Every day He calls us to serve Him by employing well the gifts He gives us. We have choices. What are we to do with the talents He gives us? We must be mindful every day, every moment even, of our response to God and the choices we make about how we use His gifts. How are we to handle and react to these blessings in our lives? Hopefully, it will be with yielded hearts that are so grateful that the only appropriate response we can make is to entrust our entire life to Jesus Christ, to be His disciple, and have the desire to act courageously and give. G K Chesterton says that "the proper form of thanks is some form of humility and restraint, and also an obedience."[16]

When I survey my life and my work, sure, I earn the money that provides the comfort of the house I live in and to enjoy the car I drive, etc. But God gave me the talent and ability to go out and earn that money. I've had a satisfying career in the financial services industry. But God gave me the interests and desire to work in that field. And God has given me the faith to acknowledge Him as the source of all I have and all I am. He has taught me in Paul's letter to Timothy not to rely on so uncertain a thing as wealth, but rather to rely on Him who richly provides everything for my enjoyment (1 Tim. 6:17-19). Therefore, I strive to choose to do good, to be rich in good works, to be generous, ready to share, and thus store up the treasure of a good foundation for the future, so as to take hold of life that really is life. I am so very blessed.

My friend Rosemarie is quick to acknowledge the blessings in her life, even in these more recent years after her husband's passing. For her and her husband, giving wasn't an option. They took it as a matter of fact—they were going to give. She told me, "It was just who we were." Her husband grew up in Cuba, and as a young married couple, they lived in Puerto Rico. So they knew the transitory nature of wealth. They moved their growing family to Miami and started a supply business. After years of struggle to get the business established, giving back was their natural response. They never questioned if they would give, or even how much to give. Their question was *where* to give. They did a lot of due diligence, making sure that the agencies they supported managed resources efficiently and spent most of their money on service to those who needed it most.

God gives us everything. All is gift. What else can we do but in overwhelming gratefulness give in ways that serve to build His kingdom, to give to those entities that do the Gospel works of mercy. Jesus is our model. How did He serve? In total submission to God. He gave His all. his very life! How do we do that? How are we to emulate Christ?

Jesus tells us how in Mark 12:31: "You shall love your neighbor as yourself." In a word, we are to love. God wants our hearts. He wants us to love Him and to love our neighbor. Love is a verb. It requires action. Love is what we do for others with our Time, Talents, and Treasure. How is Jesus calling you to love?

Pope Francis's *Gaudete et Exsultate* gives us the template:

"Be holy by living our lives with love, bearing witness in everything we do, wherever we find ourselves…the path to holiness is almost always gradual, made up of small steps in prayer, in sacrifice, and in service to others. Jesus explained with great simplicity what it means to be holy—living simply, and putting God first, trusting Him and not earthly power or wealth, being humble, mourning and consoling others, being merciful and forgiving, working for justice, and seeking peace with all."[17]

As the bishops teach, Stewardship is Discipleship—how we live our lives. Becoming a disciple of Jesus Christ leads naturally to the practice of stewardship. Each day is lived in intimate, personal relationship with the Lord.[18]

We talk about Stewardship in terms of the three T's: Time, Talent, and Treasure. Those represent the totality of all of God's gifts to us. We are to cherish them, cultivate them in responsible and accountable ways, share them with others, and return them with increase to the Lord. All of them— every moment of our Time, every bit of our Talent, and every dime of our Treasure.

This Stewardship tag-line practically rolls off the tongue, "Time, Talent, and Treasure." Notice, it is *and* Treasure, not *or*. I often hear people say that they give a lot of time volunteering at church, thinking that their volunteer work excuses them from giving money. The bishops teach that the generous sharing of resources, including money, is central to the practice of stewardship.[19]

All of us are to give from our resources, no matter how meager you think them to be. We are asked to be faithful regardless. Jesus exalted the poor widow and her two small coins in the Gospel of Mark. She provides the greatest example of trust in God's provision in that from her poverty, she gave all she had (12:41-44).

I met with a 60-something divorcee who wanted help with her budgeting. She worked as a cashier at Walmart making $13 per hour. At 40 hours per week, she could cover her living expenses, and even pay off early her one debt—an accumulated medical bill. But her scheduled hours were being cut back, sometimes to as few as 20 hours. Needless to say, that put a strain on her budget. Even so, she faithfully contributed to the church. When I asked her about that, she said, "I'll always put something in the plate. I have to give. Look at all that God has done for me."

Paul tells us in 2 Cor. 8:10-12: "For if the willingness is there, the gift is acceptable according to what one has, not according to what one doesn't have." No amount is too small. Five loaves and two fish fed thousands. God can work miracles with anything we give. But notice in John's version of this story, Jesus waited for the boy to offer up his family's bread. In turn, He waits for us to give (John 6:9). What if the boy hadn't spoken up?

Did Jesus need any help in feeding those folks on the plain? Of course not. He could have commanded filet mignon with over-stuffed baked potatoes and steamed haricot verts come down from heaven for everyone. But He waited for someone to act, someone to offer help before He then worked the miracle.

What if we don't act? Is someone missing out on a miracle because you haven't given?

....

STEWARDSHIP REFLECTION

....

Totally Dependent

The poor widow in Luke 21 didn't give much money. But it was all she had. Like Jesus on the cross, she gave everything. Her action is one of the best examples of trust and total dependence on God to provide for our very sustenance.

If the government should cut social service programs for the poor and vulnerable, will we—the Church—make up the shortfall? Will we—the Church—reflect on all the blessings in our lives, and then sacrifice and give to the poor, and trust God to meet our needs? We can if we surrender to Him and trust His lordship over every aspect of our lives. So, give. And give gladly because It's Not Your Money.

....

In Whose Image

Matthew Kelly's Dynamic Catholic Institute finds that less than 7 percent of registered parishioners donate 80 percent of financial contributions. He refers to this group as the "Highly Engaged" parishioners.[20] Rightfully, he wonders what more works of mercy could be done if the number of highly-engaged givers increased to 14 percent. He's not even invoking the Pareto Principal 80 / 20 ratio.

A Villanova University study finds a remarkably consistent result that US Catholics give at half the rate of Protestants, contributing about 1.2 percent of income compared to 2.5 percent from the typical Protestant household. The study calculates that if Catholics would raise their giving to match Protestant giving, parishes would receive another $8 billion per year![21] How many more people could be fed, clothed, housed, visited? And though that would be a doubling of giving, it still is not giving at the level of a tithe.

Why are we Catholics such pitiful givers? Is it because in the old days, taxes supported the Church, and we already pay too much in taxes? The folks in Jesus's day had that very concern. They asked Him about paying taxes in Mt. 22:15-22. I love His response to those crafty Pharisees: "Whose image is on the coin? Then pay to Caesar what belongs to Caesar and to God what belongs to God."

Some may retort, "I'm a good citizen. I pay taxes that support welfare programs. I go to Mass almost every week. I'm a lector and I volunteer. I put $20 in the plate. That is enough." It isn't. That is compartmentalized thinking. Let me ask you to step back for a moment and consider—what belongs to God? In the quiet moments of your day while in prayer and reflection, do you acknowledge God as the Giver of all that you are and all that you have? Is He first in every area of your life? Do your actions throughout the day reflect that belief? Are you made in Caesar's image or in God's image? Is God's image engraved on your heart? Because where our hearts are is where we keep our treasure (Mt. 6:21).

Is our meager giving due to concerns about the overall leadership, management, and operations of the Church? I'd be remiss if I didn't mention the diabolical scandal that plagues the Church today. In many ways, Church leadership has demonstrated that it is less than transparent and trustworthy. Maybe giving should be reduced or even withheld. Lower offertory amounts might get the clergy's attention and force the institution to be more forthcoming and accountable for its actions, right? Wrong.

While there are legitimate concerns for how the bishops manage all the various challenges facing the Church, discontinuing our giving is the wrong answer to the scandal issue. Besides, Catholics were the lowest of givers well before the scandal. And, giving is too important to our individual spirituality to wield generosity as a weapon threatening the Church with slicing and dicing our checks as with a knife.

Consider these seven thoughts on the spirituality of giving:

- Giving and Blessing are gifts from God. God is a giver. As disciples, we should strive to be like Him. Whenever we give, we are being like Him. When our giving is sacrificial—a bit uncomfortable and for the benefit of others—then in our small-scale way, we approach the sacrificial self-giving of Jesus on the cross. Our giving becomes a way of preaching the Gospel.

- When we give, we experience a unique closeness to God, our Father, that only comes to us as we are generous. Like all parents, God wants to see His children being kind and generous and loving. God loves a cheerful giver (2 Cor. 9:7).

- Obedience to God's commands to give is our intentional acknowledgement of His authority in our lives. He is entitled to honor and respect. His divine lordship over every facet of our lives, including our money, is not a threat, but a place of safety and security.

- Giving is a concrete manifestation of our faith and trust in God to provide: "Let your lives be free from the love of money, but be content with what you have, for he has said, 'I will never forsake you or abandon you'" (Heb. 13:5).

- Giving makes us active participants in the mission of the Church. It makes us a part of something larger, more majestic, and holier than ourselves: "Please help them in a way worthy of God...to support such persons so that we may be co-workers in the truth" (3 John 6-8).

- Sacrificial giving is self-denial. It is laying our worldly desires at the foot of the cross, and there receiving God's grace, mercy, and forgiveness: "Beloved, I urge you as aliens and sojourners to keep away from worldly desires that wage war against the soul" (1 Pet. 2:11).

- Giving is an act of praise and worship of our God. It is one of the best expressions of gratitude we can make for all the blessings God gives to us.

FRUIT OF THE SPIRIT

CHARITY

*The biblical ideal of caring for the neediest people
of the community. Love. Self-giving.*[22]

Mt. 25:40
"Whatever you did for one of these least brothers of mine, you did for me."

James 1:27
"Religion that is pure and undefiled before God the Father is this: to care for orphans and widows."

1 John 3:18
"Children, let us love not in word or in speech, but in deed and truth."

So please give for your spiritual wellbeing. Be courageous. Be charitable in order to live a holy life in imitation of Christ. Give out of gratefulness for all the blessings and benefits God gives to you. Give in obedience to God's Word, and so discover a peace and freedom you can't find anywhere else.

If you are in Matthew Kelly's "Highly Engaged" group of givers, thank you for your witness. Even so, is your giving from surplus or is it a sacrifice? If you give in amounts less than a tithe, what are the obstacles that keep you from giving what the Bible commands? How might your life be different if you did give in obedience to God's Word? If you are in the 40 percent of non-givers, how do you reconcile that with all the blessings God bestows on you? How can you take that step of faith, begin to give, and be a part of such a transformative force? You could literally change the world.

Okay, that's a lot. Take a breath. Then please read on to learn the "how-to's," how to do it. How can you align your personal finances with God's way, and so be a part of such a transformative force in our world?

"We make a living by what we get;
we make a life by what we give."

Winston Churchill

CHAPTER THREE

Seek Heaven and Gain All Else Besides

I want to. How do I?

That was tough! As I forewarned. Pursuing anything worthwhile is difficult and demanding. You know that. I've been praying for you to persevere. If you are still reading, my prayers have been answered. You should now be asking how to implement financial stewardship as a way of life. And just as in anticipation of the start of a recital, or to the kick-off to begin the big game, you may have a few jitters. That's okay.

The story of little Johnny and the cookie jar fits well here. You've probably heard it before how Johnny's mom put freshly baked home-made chocolate chip cookies into the cookie jar just as Johnny came in from school. She told him in no uncertain terms, "Johnny, I am going to freshen up. Don't you dare take a cookie from the cookie jar."

You know what Johnny did.

Upon her return, Mom noticed the cookie jar's lid askew and crumbs on the counter. She asked, "Johnny, did you take a cookie?" Furtive eyes, a quivering lip, and sweat beads across his brow announced the truth of Johnny's actions. There was probably a butterfly or two fluttering in his stomach. When you think about God's priority for handling finances and how tithing will fit into your budget, is there a fluttering in your stomach? Do you break out in a cold sweat? That's what happened to me. As I said earlier, I knew a lot of passages about tithing from my Baptist days. Yet, I wasn't doing what I knew I was supposed to do. It gnawed at me. Why wasn't I willing to try God in this and bring the whole tithe into the storehouse (Mal. 3:10)? Taking that first step of purposefully giving more was gutwrenching. It was like Indiana Jones facing that big step out into the abyss in order to cross the chasm and get to the Holy Grail.

At this juncture you may be saying, "Okay, I get it. But really, how much am I supposed to give? How do I take that step of faith? I usually put $20 in the plate. You just told me the national average is $10, so I'm doing my part. More than most, even. And anyway, $20 is close to what it cost us last night to go out for a meal at a fast-casual restaurant. That's tastier and more relaxing than Mass, but it's church after all. So, $20 seems about right. Right?"

First off, that'd be $20 per person at almost any decent eatery. But hey, I used to give $20 per week, too. That's $1000 per year, a meaningful amount. If giving $20 puts you in a similar position as the widow in Mark 12, then it might be the right amount, maybe even too much. I don't think God wants you to take food away from your children or cause you to miss paying a utility bill. If, on the other hand, your giving is a reactionary whatever-happens-to-be-in-your-pocket, out of your surplus, then the amount probably needs some re-examination. King David said in 2 Sam. 24:24, "I cannot sacrifice to the Lord my God burnt offerings that cost me nothing." If your giving doesn't really cost you, if you don't really feel it, you'd be wise to consider if the amount correlates to the full measure of God's blessings in your life.

So how much to give, then? The Old Testament is clear in its command to give 10 percent from first fruits. Many people wonder that, since we are Christians, do we hold to the Old Testament law. Fair question. I proposed in Chapter 2 that it is the spirit of the law that should guide us. We get a sense of the spirit of the law by a couple of giving examples in the New Testament. We looked at

Zacchaeus's story summarized in Chapter 2. He gave half his wealth. John the Baptist preached in Luke 3:11 that whoever has two tunics should share one. Call that 50 percent giving. Jesus told the rich young man in Mt. 19 to sell everything. That's 100 percent. Jesus gave His life—all in! Again, I think the spirit of the law calls for being detached from money and material things and giving generously and courageously without expecting anything back.

"Joe, I hear you. That all sounds good, but what is the answer? How much from us? Is it 10 percent as a matter of law, because the spirit of the law seems to ask too much?" I've actually had people ask me, "Is it to be from gross income or net? Or from the total value of all assets?" "Do in-kind contributions count?" "If it is not tax deductible, does it count as a charitable contribution?" "If good feelings come from giving, does it count?" I honestly don't think God gets bogged down in this minutia. I think He only cares about our intentions, our willingness to give and trust Him.

Back in Chapter 2, I quoted 2 Cor. 8:10-12 where Paul tells us we are to give according to what we have, not according to what we don't have. A couple of teachings in the Catechism may help here. Paragraph 1351 says, "Those who are well off, and who are also willing, give as each chooses. What is gathered is given to him who presides to assist orphans and widows, those whom illness or any other cause has deprived of resources, prisoners, immigrants and, in a word, all who are in need." And again, Paragraph 2043 says, "The faithful also have the duty of providing for the material needs of the Church, each according to his abilities."

But back to the question of how much is the right amount for you to give. For the answer, truly you should submit to God in prayer. Seek His will for your life and how He wants you to obey His teachings as they apply to your finances. The Old Testament teaches the tithe, which is 10 percent. Getting started, even in baby steps, is vital to your spiritual growth. How much do you spend on mercy versus how much on luxuries? Add up how much of your monthly bills go for electronic entertainment: cable TV, internet access, cell phone, Netflix, etc. Shouldn't God get at least that amount? What's important is not so much the amount, but that your giving is done willingly and in genuine response to the blessings in your life.

The pastor who led me through RCIA so many years ago provided one of the best answers I've ever gotten on this subject. He taught that the amount I give is between me and God. But whatever the amount, it should be "sacrificial." He defined a sacrificial amount as that number at the very edge of my resources. An amount I'm not sure I can afford to give. An amount that forces me to trust in God to help me make it. An amount that is reflective of how intimate I wish my relationship with God to be. Giving an amount that is sacrificial accentuates the sacred over the secular.[23]

I had a conversation about this with a fellow parishioner. He told me how much he put into the basket. I commented that that number added up to a pretty good amount. And then I asked, "What percentage of your income is that?" He asked in return, "I haven't thought about that. Why is that important?" I told him about Bible passages that speak to giving 10 percent. He said, "10 percent, huh?" I could see him do a quick calculation. "That much? Really?" When I went on to share that the Church teaches giving a sacrificial gift, a light bulb went off in his head. He exclaimed, "Oh, you're talking about Faith Giving!" Faith giving. I love that.

Tithing depends on trust. Trust comes from faith. Faith is a gift. Pray for the gift of faith to trust and give.

FRUIT OF THE SPIRIT

FAITHFULNESS

To trust in and rely on God. Fidelity to God is the sign of the righteous person. Faith is dynamic, an activity that manifests itself in love.[24]

Examples: **ABRAHAM and MARY**
Abraham had faith that God would provide the sacrifice.
Mary had faith in what Gabriel told her.
Both heard the message, believed it, and acted upon it.

CCC 222 and 227

Believing in God, and loving Him with all our being has enormous consequences for our whole life.

- It means coming to know God's greatness and majesty.

- It means living in thanksgiving.

- It means knowing the true dignity of all people.

- It means making good use of created things.

- It means trusting God in every circumstance.

Practical Applications

As Christian Stewards, we should joyfully acknowledge God who so richly provides our everything. We should demonstrate that by embodying an attitude of generosity, sharing our Time, Talent, and Treasure with our most needy and vulnerable neighbors. Trusting God and not worrying about the future, we should have no concern about building cash reserves for emergencies or saving for college or retirement. Live for today and let tomorrow take care of itself, right?

Not exactly. We certainly should live in the present. Tomorrow has enough of its own troubles (Mt. 6:34). But we surely should be prudent in our spending and saving decisions. Proverbs 21:5 says, "The plans of the diligent end in profit, but those of the hasty end in loss." And verse 21:20 gives a sense of the results of planning: "Precious treasure and oil are in the house of the wise, but the fool consumes them." You know the story of Joseph who was sold off to Egypt as a slave but then rose to be put in charge of all the land. He implemented a savings plan that helped the Egyptians live through the coming famine (Gen. 41).

Planning is important. The danger is an attitude of presumption. The Catechism defines two kinds of presumption in Paragraph 2092. First, it is an over-reliance on God's power and thus, not acting with the talents He gives. Second, it is an over-reliance on our own abilities, assuming we don't need His help. If we are so certain of ourselves, of what we'll be able to do and accomplish and pay back, we risk being like the folks in the book of James saying, "Today we shall go do such-and-such and make a profit." James rightly accuses them of boasting in their arrogance. We, too, need to check ourselves and admit we really have no idea what tomorrow holds, that we "are like a puff of smoke that appears briefly, then disappears" (4:13-17).

Planning is indispensable. Thinking about and asking the Holy Spirit for guidance about our future is vital and good. Jesus tells us to sit down and calculate the costs before beginning a project or waging a campaign (Luke 14:25-33). But, as with any project or campaign, there are many variables, and uncontrollable and unforeseen possibilities. It is OK to have plans, but when those plans hit reality, be prepared to change. As Mike Tyson might tell you, a plan is great until you get punched in the face. He has to press on and adapt, and so do we. As we strive to implement the plan, we need to be open to the Holy Spirit's guidance and adapt as we go. We need to be tentative about our plans so that God has room to intervene and act. James speaks to us as he corrects those folks in Chapter 4, verse 15 to say, "If the Lord wills it, we shall go and do...."

So as the Lord wills it, how are we to manage our resources in ways that glorify God? This section is not meant to be a full exploration of the principles of sound financial planning practice that incorporates all of the steps of a comprehensive financial planning engagement. For our purposes, we will review some rules-of-thumb to see how the secular industry's applications may relate to our effort at Christian stewardship. To get started, here are a few commonly accepted guidelines:

- Have 6 to 12 months of expenses in savings for emergencies.

- Have life insurance death benefits equal to 10 to 15 times annual salary.

- And have 8 times annual salary saved and invested by age 60 in order to confidently expect to replace 60 percent of income in retirement.

Reaching these mileposts frequently requires big numbers. Hitting them often necessitates savings levels and insurance costs well beyond current cash-flow capacities. Such planning results can scare people into a feeling of futility that propagates paralysis. People in that situation end up so confused that they never take the needed action to work toward the important goals and objectives that will protect them now and in the future. What good is that? Having emergency cash reserves and life insurance are important. Saving for those twilight days when, as a seasoned citizen, you may not be able to earn the same income as you did in your peak earning years is also important. You must take action now, even if limited action, to work toward these goals.

Good stewardship unquestionably requires making provisions for family needs. 1 Tim. 5:8 says, "Whoever does not provide for relatives and especially family members has denied the faith and is worse than an unbeliever." But how much is enough? We talked earlier about providing for the true needs of family versus spending on lifestyle choices. How to define the needs? By taking it to God in prayer. Absolutely include your spouse and talk to other godly people you trust whose counsel will help you get a sense of how your needs align with your Ideals. That will lead to understanding the appropriate action steps you need to take for your unique situation.

Saving and investing are important, but only when also giving alms. If we leave out almsgiving and focus solely on saving and investing for ourselves, we can become inordinately drawn to selfishness and greed. Our hearts will be where our treasure is (Mt. 6:21).

A colleague told me of a spending decision he and his wife made that is a great example of combining personal needs with the needs of others. He commuted 60 miles per day driving an old but paid-for SUV. So, he traded that vehicle in for a newer, smaller car which got close to 30 miles per gallon. Even with the car loan, he spent less than the cost of fuel for that thirsty SUV. Good stewardship, he thought. Then, a friend called to tell of his entry into the mission field. He was seeking support and needed $300 per month. That just happened to be the amount of my colleague's car note. The couple decided to trade back the newer car for an older sedan they could pay for outright. That freed up the money they were spending on the car payment to instead give to their friend's mission needs. And as it turned out, my colleague's office location soon was reassigned much closer to their home. Amazing how things work out.

FRUIT OF THE SPIRIT

SELF-CONTROL
The practice of self-denial for spiritual reasons. Asceticism.

Example: **ST. AUGUSTINE**
Temperance is a disposition that restrains our desire for things which it is base to desire.

CCC 2340
Whoever wants to remain faithful to their baptismal promises and resist temptation will want to adopt the means for doing so.

CCC 1734
The practice of self-denial is one such means. Giving alms, praying, and fasting are other means. Such efforts enhance the mastery of the will over its acts.

CCC 1809
Temperance is the moral virtue that moderates the attraction of pleasures and provides balance in the use of created goods.

2 Tm. 4:5
But you be self-possessed in all circumstances.

Titus 2:12
Live sober, upright, and godly lives in this world.

Where do you begin to figure out how all this can work for you? As you undoubtedly know, the best tool for calculating and planning the management of our Treasure is —(drum roll)—a budget.

Budgeting

Ta-dah! There it is. Budget (groan!). The very word connotes drudgery, anxiety, fear and fighting. A major cause of marital problems is financial strain. The budgeting process facilitates communication between spouses. Therefore, budgets are seriously important tools for families and, of course, for individuals. They enable thoughtful consideration of financial priorities and opportunities to submit spending decisions to God in prayer.

Many resources exist for budgets and budgeting guidance. A quick Google search for the word "budgeting" revealed 279 million hits. *Your Money Counts* devotes a very helpful chapter to budgeting.[25] Credit Union members often enjoy free expert help with budgeting. My son the engineer uses the Tiller application.

Compass Catholic Ministries offers an excellent budget spreadsheet on its website www.compasscatholic.org. It is at the "Resources" tab under "Financial Spreadsheets" and entitled "Estimated Spending Plan." As stewards, God is first in all things, so the Estimated Spending Plan puts Giving and Tithing in the number one slot of expenses. Saving and Investing come after obligatory taxes. Following are line-items of particulars for those who want to dig deep. This spreadsheet presents a traditional approach to budgeting. It is very good for those who want to get into the details.

Another budgeting technique is to assign percentages of income for each category of spending. If you've ever applied for a mortgage, you know that lenders want your mortgage payment to be less than 28 percent of your income. When insurance, taxes, utilities, and maintenance are added in, total housing expenses should come to less than 40 percent of income.

Chapter 14 of Your Money Counts provides a good example of percentage guidelines as follows:

Giving / Saving / Investing	20%
Housing	30-40%
Food	5-15%
Transportation	10-15%
Clothing	2-7%
Medical / Health	5-10%
Education	2-7%
Personal	5-10%
Entertainment / Vacation	5-10%
Debts (except mortgage)	0-10%

I personally don't want to spend a lot of time managing spreadsheets and balancing check books. I know myself well enough to know I don't want to delve into the minutiae of where every penny is spent. I changed my major in college from Accounting to Finance for just that reason. So, the system I use at home is what I call the "Don't Worry About It" budget. It is based on the soundest of financial and Biblical principles. I learned it from Mr. John Smith, my algebra teacher in high school. Mr. Smith was a deacon at his Baptist church and a long-time Sunday School teacher. He would often hold the first five minutes of class for devotional time. One particular series was on the topic of tithing. In the course of a few days he shared a most profound, but amazingly simple, formula for financial success. "Foolproof," he called it. Works all the time, every time, no matter the scenario. It is this:

10 / 10 / 80

GIVE 10% of income

SAVE 10% of income

LIVE on 80%

Once my late wife and I decided to tithe, we rearranged our budget to this formula. I trusted Mr. Smith's advice, and he was right. It just works. Worry about money flew out the window, like a trapped fly released once the car window is cracked open.

Giving 10% of income to church and charity
= Peace knowing we are following God's commands in the Bible.

Saving/Investing 10% of income
= Peace knowing we are building funds for short-term emergencies and long-term goals.

Living on 80% of income
= Freedom from worry about spending knowing that the most important priorities are being addressed.

This may sound simplistic. It is. I know from having worked as a Financial Planning Practitioner that we can make things complicated sometimes. And certainly, some client situations are complicated. But for most people, it really is this simple. If you are not a detail person, I strongly encourage you to give this "Don't Worry About It" budget a try. In so doing, you put God first and trust Him to provide by tithing ten percent right off the top. Then, arrange for deductions from paychecks to go to a savings account and your 401k or IRA for another ten percent. The remaining 80 percent is free to spend on lifestyle choices. This is a great technique to start on the path toward managing your money God's way.

....

GIFT OF THE SPIRIT

....

WISDOM
The pursuit of a lifestyle of proper ethical conduct.
A gift to be asked of from God.[26]

Example: **SOLOMON'S WISDOM**
But Jesus's wisdom is greater than Solomon's (Luke 11: 31).

CCC 1831
A gift of the Holy Spirit which helps complete and perfect the virtues of those who receive them.

Prv. 16:16
"How much better to get Wisdom than gold."

Prv. 30:8-9
"Give me neither poverty nor riches, provide me only with what I need, lest being full, I deny you."

Eccl. 7:12
"For the protection of Wisdom is as the protection of money."

Wis. 8:5
"If riches are desirable in life, what is richer than wisdom who produces all things?"

....

Whether using a detailed spreadsheet, guided by general category percentages, or engaging the "Don't Worry About It" budget, what will you do if the bottom line is negative? You really have only two options: increase income or reduce expenses. Maybe you could work a second job. But consider first what can you do to cut expenses. And with student loans and consumer credit at record levels, is it debt service that's driving your budget into a brick wall?

Debt Management

Should you even carry any debt? While owing money does presume upon the future and your ability to pay back the debt owed, Scripture does not specifically call debt a sin. It does, however, strongly discourage debt. We read in Proverbs 22:7, "The rich rule over the poor, and the borrower is the slave of the lender." Think about that for a minute; when you borrow, you become a slave to the lender. What is it like to be a slave? A slave has absolutely no freedom. He cannot do what he wants, but must do what his master wants him to do, even if it is uncomfortable and distasteful. Borrowed money must be paid back. You are obligated to make payments, no matter what else is going on in your home and work life. You have no choice but to generate the needed income or cut expenses in order to have the ability to pay the debt. You are no longer free, and the resources you might have had to do good and build God's kingdom are necessarily diverted to pay the lender/master.

Studies done by Quicken Loans and Nerd Wallet estimate average credit card debt for households that carry over balances month-to-month range between $8,300 and $15,200. Add to that the average auto loan of $27,800 and student loans at a whopping $46,800 and you can see that Americans are drowning in a sea of debt. Repaying those obligations is what enslaves us and hinders our ability to serve God more freely.

My VISA card charges 16.99% on any balance outstanding over 30 days. If I carried the average $8,300 balance, I'd pay $1,410 per year in interest. WOW! What else could that $1,410 per year do? What if instead, I gave $210 to God which then would allow me to invest $1200—a nice, round number of $100 per month? If my investment could earn 7 percent per year, over 20 years it could grow to over $49,000; over 30 years it could be over $113,000. I'd rather have that in my wallet than lose it to the credit card company.

If you have debt, how do you eliminate it as quickly as possible to get out of slavery? There is a tried-and-true strategy that I learned back in the 1980's when training to work as a financial planner. It's been around a long time because it is effective. The strategy calls for listing debts from smallest to the largest amounts owed. The goal is to pay off that smallest debt first by whatever means necessary to get that done. Start by paying just the minimum payments on all the other debts and adding the overpayments from those other debts to the smallest. You may also need to sell off assets and/or reduce cash reserves (but not to zero) and apply those funds to the smallest debt. Again, whatever is required to do, get rid of that smallest balance. Once eliminated, apply that debt's payment combined with all the other debt's overpayments now to the second debt to pay it off as soon as possible. When paid off, take what was paid on the second debt and add it to the third debt's payment. And so on.

This strategy is commonly called "snowballing your debt." Like a snowball, it starts small, and gets bigger as payments from smaller debts now paid off are applied to larger debts, and eventually the payment snowball overcomes the debt burden. Scooping up a bucketful of snow and molding it into a ball is not hard to do. Hence, the strategy calls for starting with the smallest debt. But dedication to paying off all your debt is hard. It requires grit and determination, just as pushing a waist-high ball of snow requires strenuous effort. Imagine, however, the feeling you'll have when the size of your snowball debt payments overwhelms and pays off all your debt—Eureka! Euphoria! What a sense of relief and accomplishment.

A visual of snowballing your debt is below:

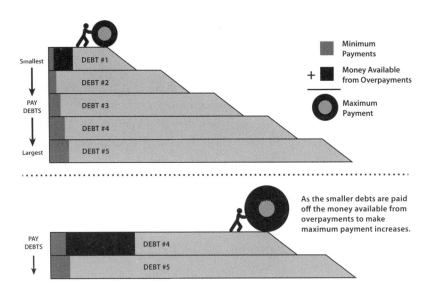

Make the commitment today to get all your debt paid off. In doing so, you will experience a sense of freedom and gain new opportunities to redirect cash flow to the higher rewards of building God's kingdom.

My friend Tom shared with me about a difficult year he had experienced. He was living the good life. He earned a six-figure income, as did his wife. They had no concern about how they spent. Big house with a pool. Boat. Third car. A sports car, of course. Ate out almost every night. Traveled when and where they wanted. Not a concern in the world. Until he lost his job. Then he lost his marriage. Then he lost everything. "Being Lord of my life wasn't working too well for me," said Tom. And so began his quest back to the Church.

During that quest, he started to utilize a budget and snowballed his debt. He now lives a simpler lifestyle, spending below his income, and his only debt is a mortgage. "I truly have no concerns now. I remember Father's New Year's sermon. Three words: 'God—Will—Provide.' And man, does He."

STEWARDSHIP REFLECTION

Is your world upside down? Lost your job? Investment accounts down? House not worth what you owe on it? Wish things could go back to how they were?

Jeremiah exhorts us in Chapter 3 to think of it no longer, nor remember it, nor miss it. Of course, he was preaching to the Jews in exile who longed for the day when they could go see the Ark of the Covenant. That exile helped them to see that God is not contained in a box. He is relentlessly everywhere in our lives.

In difficult times, do not look nostalgically to the past, but ask God what He wants you to do now.

Now that you have chosen to put God first and give, you have to choose worthy recipients. We must be discerning. Obviously, there are many deserving causes, and you probably can't support them all in any meaningful and impactful way. So how do you decide who to give to and how much to give? Brueggeman tells us that, "Deuteronomy is insistent that money and possessions must be managed in the practice of justice, that is, for the good of the entire community."[27] Thus, pray to discover ministries that do good, that serve the community. Pray for guidance to align your giving with your values and priorities. Seek counsel from trusted friends and advisors. And consider this suggested formula for giving, often published in Bishops Annual Appeal literature. The guidelines recommend giving 5 percent to your home Parish, 1 percent to the Appeal, and 4 percent to other charities.

In seeking out worthy charities, look for a compelling mission and a clear vision. How do their values mesh with yours? What causes are important to you? For me, it is important that they serve the most vulnerable among us—the homeless, young unwed mothers-to-be, the elderly, and those living below the poverty line. I look for ministries that educate and protect children, especially the unborn. When I find them, I then want to know about their financial stewardship. Transparency is paramount. The ministries' financial reporting must demonstrate how the vast majority of my contributions will go to serve their clients and how relatively little goes to administrative costs.

I am lucky to be a member of a parish that does tremendous outreach to the poor and underserved. That makes it easy to give the majority of my tithe to my church, knowing that most of the money goes to feed the hungry and educate kids, many of whom live in households that earn below the poverty line. Our church also has a housing ministry, and provides medical and transportation assistance and many other services that poor people need. Of course, Catholic Charities and St. Vincent DePaul are excellent choices, too. For non-church charities, here are three sources to help you discover the information you need to make informed choices: BBB Wise Giving Alliance, Charity Navigator, and Charity Watch. Review their websites to learn if your chosen charity meets prudent stewardship standards.

Mission statements and financial reports are easy enough to evaluate before writing checks payable to non-profit charities. I struggle more when it comes to responding to cash requests on the street. I find Matthew Kelly's Dynamic Catholic website offers good suggestions for every day, street-level generosity: "Every time you give to someone, challenge yourself to go just a bit further. If you are about to write a check for $20, how about make it $25. If you're going to donate a coat, throw in a scarf, too. If you want to buy a homeless person a cup of coffee, add in a sandwich. If you challenge yourself to stretch just a bit more out of your comfort zone, you will grow in your generosity. Remember, generosity is about so much more than doling out money or material goods. It is primarily an attitude and a way of being. By intentionally practicing regular acts of giving and sharing, you will indeed become a more generous person—and be all the happier for it."[28]

Generosity is a disposition, and budgeting is a process. Both require commitment and communication. Talk with your spouse, or, if you're single, speak with other counsel you trust about your spending priorities and your goals and objectives. Pray about this. Plan your finances with a budget using this 10 / 10 / 80 formula. Be intentional. Be a good steward. Give on purpose. Save on purpose. Eliminate worry.

Stewardship doesn't just happen. Discipleship has a cost. Jesus tells us in Luke 9:23-24 that if we want to follow Him, we must deny ourselves and pick up our cross daily. We must be intentional; the cost of stewardship is intentionality. You must take the time and make the effort to put God first—to read the Bible, to pray, to worship, and to serve. And with your finances, you must plan and budget, or otherwise your spending will be haphazard at best, out of control at worst. The world, through various media, puts too many enticing obstacles in our way. We must be diligent disciples and stewards in cultivating our gifts of Time and Talent and sharing our Treasure.

I sat with a lady during the lunch break at a Women's Conference where I presented an It's Not Your Money™ workshop. Her story is a great example of intentionality and trust. She told me, "I need the grace of tithing." That struck me, so I asked her to elaborate. She shared that being self-employed, her and her husband's income was erratic. Knowing how dependent they were on God, they established their weekly giving through EFT drafts. That way, no matter what, God was paid first.

She told me that some months they'd be down to the last $20 in their checking account, not knowing where the next paycheck would come from or when. She'd just put it in the collection plate. She'd cry out, "God, this is from you. I give it back to you." And then with a twinkle and a tear in her eye, she said that the next job would come, or a check would arrive in the mailbox. "Isn't God amazing?!" Indeed.

....

STEWARDSHIP REFLECTION

....

Give Lavishly

Psalm 112 says those who fear the Lord are blessed and generous. They give lavishly to the poor.

Hasn't God given to us lavishly? Does He not lavish us with mercy, forgiveness, and peace? Are not our talents and abilities given to us so that we are able to serve and prosper?

In response, we are to be generous. We are to exude joy. We are to give lavishly to the poor. We are to give because It's Not Our Money.

....

In Chapter 2, I asked, "What are you working for?" The same could be asked of your budget plan: "What are you saving and investing for?" What are your long-term goals and objectives? How do those change at various stages in your life? And especially for Baby Boomers, what are your objectives toward the end of life? What I mean by that is what legacy do you want to leave to your loved ones?

Legacy is more than leaving money. Legacy in this context is about communicating important lessons and values about life and money that you want to live beyond you. The starting point to answer this question is your Ideal. The highest Ideal is to be holy, to imitate Christ. How will you communicate that to your loved ones when you pass on to your glory?

One means of communicating your legacy is to write a "Legacy Letter." This letter enlightens and confirms for your loved ones what is important to you about your faith, about how to be and how to live, and why you believe those things. It can be an old-fashioned written document. It can be a video or podcast. Whatever and however you choose to transmit your message, what a tremendous gift to leave for your family.

To get started, take out a piece of paper and answer these questions:

- What do you believe about Jesus? Who is Jesus to you?
- How has God blessed you in your life?
- How has the Church community supported and helped you along the way?
- What is the most important lesson or message you want pass along?
- What assurances can you give? What wishes and desires do you have for your family?

While a Legacy Letter passes on your spirit and your heart, it does not specifically address financial matters. Those particulars are best addressed in your estate documents, as well as how accounts are titled, and how beneficiaries are named in life insurance and retirement investment accounts. Financial legacy deals more with account ownership and the legal documents that determine how your assets will flow through to your loved ones. The question is how much money do you want your family to inherit?

Digging deeper into that question, consider if we should even be concerned about the kids inheriting anything. If we practice good stewardship, we cultivate our gifts, share them with others, and return them with increase to the Lord. If we return our gifts to the Lord, should we care about leaving an inheritance for our family?

Over the many years of my financial service work, I've heard answers to this question at both extremes and everywhere in between. Some want to leave so much to their kids, they'll buy extra life insurance just to accomplish that. Others will glibly say that the last thing they want to hear when their dead body hits the pavement is change jingling in their pockets. What does God say? Look at Proverbs 13:22:

"The good leave an inheritance to their children's children." And 2 Cor. 12:14 reads, "Children ought not to save for their parents, but parents for their children."

So surely, we should want to leave something for our kids and grandchildren to inherit. But how much? Proverbs also says in 20:21, "An estate quickly acquired in the beginning will not be blessed in the end." 1 Tm. 6:17 speaks to this: "As for those who in this present age are rich, commend them not to be haughty or to set their hopes on the uncertainty of riches." If loved ones would become rich through inheritance, should we want to put them in such a position? *Your Money Counts* cites a quote by Andrew Carnegie: "The almighty dollar bequeathed to a child is a mighty curse."[29]

I had to grapple with this very issue after my first wife died. While she was alive, and especially when we were younger, I had a large amount of life insurance so that if I died, she'd have enough to cover the children's education and other expenses and to carry on herself. But, now that she's passed, do my kids need to inherit that much life insurance? The short answer—no.

My children are now educated adults. By God's grace, I've provided them everything they need to be faithful, productive, successful citizens. I do want them to inherit some money from my estate, but only if I haven't needed it for my own medical or assisted-living needs, should those expenses be necessary. The last thing I would want is for my kids to have to pay for my long-term care needs. Any money available over and above all of that, I want to go to my favorite charities.

And that brings us full circle back to legacy. My children know by the way we've lived our lives how important my church community is to me. They know that God is the first priority in my life. They know the 10/10/80 budget formula (whether they apply it or not). When I die, they will experience firsthand how important it is to me that my resources go to charities that do the Gospel works of mercy in addition to my family.

I asked you in the Ideal section about reviewing your schedule and your checkbook. For legacy purposes I now ask,

If I reviewed your estate planning documents and your beneficiary designations, would I see evidence that God is first in your life?

"Riches can prick us with a thousand troubles
in getting them, as many cares in preserving them,
more anxieties in spending them, and
with grief in losing them."

St. Francis de Sales

CHAPTER FOUR

Peace Beyond Understanding

I will. What's in it for me?

You now have the basics of how to manage your financial resources in ways that conform to God's commands. If I were to condense these to one simple instruction, it boils down to this: Give. Give. Give. Giving is the solution to all your financial problems. Is that the message of this book? Not entirely, but it is about giving. Why? Because giving is important to our spirituality. Giving produces consequences that are among the great mysteries of our faith. Think of the Prayer of St. Francis, from which the song "Make Me a Channel of Your Peace" comes: in pardoning we are pardoned, in dying we are raised to eternal life, and in giving we receive. Giving is its own reward. By giving, we receive the truest sense of peace and joy. Isn't that what we all want—peace, contentment, fulfillment?

Another major theme of this book is the freedom that comes as result of obedience to God's Word. The prophet Jeremiah instructs us to walk in the way of God's commands so that it will be well with us (Jer.7:23). Being well means contentment and fulfillment. Being well brings the blessing of peace.

Yet another theme is detachment from material things. Consumerism and materialism cause us to be overly affixed to things, which brings about the tyranny of greed and worry. Greed and worry distract us from our Ideal and zap our time and energy to build God's kingdom here and now. Detachment, on the other hand, declutters our life and shifts our focus away from ourselves to doing works of mercy for others. It changes us to be more concerned about serving than getting, which results in reduced worry over money. Do you worry?

Working in the investment and financial planning industry my entire career, I've encountered a lot of people who worry about money. Their salaries ranged from $50,000 to $500,000. They may have saved up $30,000, $300,000 or $3,000,000. It didn't really matter. They still worried. Heck, sometimes I worry about money. In the cacophony of everyday life there are plenty of opportunities to worry.

Let's review a few culprits:

- Financial planning advice has been to buy a house and take on a mortgage payment that is just beyond what one can afford today. The pressure on the budget should be temporary because raises and promotions will increase income in the future and housing prices always go up, right?
- The generational squeeze requires us to juggle the financial demands of providing for elderly parents while saving for children's college expenses and also trying to save for retirement.
- Advertisers convince us of all the stuff we need to make us happy. No worries about the cost as long as the monthly payment is manageable. Besides, credit card companies are all too quick to offer yet another card to accommodate those purchases.
- Debt and the resulting payments pile up to beyond what we can afford.
- These are on top of time-stretched schedules busy with kids' after-school activities with no time to cook. Thus, we eat out more often, which increases our spending on food. And this on top of buying double mocha lattes on the way to work and needing the latest and greatest technology gadgets. All of these work together to squeeze our budgets and add stress to our lives.

The volatility of the stock market and its reaction to news events also create opportunities to worry:

- The Seventies had oil shocks, stagflation, and the Vietnam War.
- The Eighties saw double-digit interest rates, and Black Monday.
- In the 2000's (the "Oh-Oh's" as I like to call them) we had a tech bubble crash and a financial collapse.
- We have weathered Brexit and Grexit, Democrats and Republicans, rate hikes and tapering, fiscal cliffs and government shutdowns. And as I write this, the coronavirus pandemic.

So, yes, there is often much to worry about. Except God tells us not to worry. In Matthew 6:25-34 Jesus tells us four times to stop worrying:

Verse 25
"Do not worry about your life, what you will eat, drink, or wear."

Verse 27
"Can you add a single year to your life by worrying?"

Verse 31
"Therefore, do not worry."

Verse 34
"So, do not worry about your life tomorrow."

Why do we worry so much? In Matthew 6:33, Jesus tells us that if we strive for the Kingdom of God, all we need will be given to us. We know of His feeding thousands on the plain with just a few loaves and fish. There were twelve baskets left over (Mark 6:34-44). He commanded ravens to feed Elijah during a three-year drought (1 Kings 17:1-4). He provided the sacrifice for Abraham and so spared Isaac (Gen. 22:1-14). He knows us intimately—when we sit and stand, what we speak, where we go. He encircles us front and back (Psalm 139). He feeds the birds and clothes the lilies of the field. Are we not worth more to Him than they (Mt. 6:26-30)? Why are we of so little faith? Why do we worry? It boils down to trust. Do we trust God to provide?

What does God promise if we obey His commands to give? We can trust that...

He loves us. We are important to Him.

Mt. 10:28-31

Do not be afraid; are not two sparrows sold for a small coin? Yet not one of them falls to the ground without your Father's knowledge. You are worth more than many sparrows.

He protects us. He cares for us.

Mark 4:39-40

He woke up and rebuked the wind, "Quiet. Be still." Then He asked, "Why are you terrified? Do you not yet have faith?"

He will never leave our side.

Heb. 13:5

"Let your life be free from the love of money but be content with what you have, for He said, 'I will never forsake you or abandon you.'"

We are blessed when we trust.

Jer. 17:7-8

"Blessed are those who trust in the Lord; the Lord will be their trust. They are like a tree planted beside the waters that stretches out its roots to the stream. It does not fear heat when it comes, its leaves stay green; in the year of drought it shows no distress."

Psalm 128:1-2

"Blessed are those who fear the Lord, who walk in the his ways. What your hands provide you will enjoy; You will be happy and prosper."

He gives good gifts.

Mt. 7:8-11

If you then who are wicked know how to give good gifts to your children, how much more will your heavenly Father give good things to those who ask Him.

What are those good things that God gives? What do blessings look like? Giving is not a tit-for-tat bargain proposition whereby we tithe and so get even more money or other worldly benefits commonly believed to display success. God may choose to provide earthly, material rewards, or He may not. He may choose to allow wonderful relationships and good health, or not. It is totally up to Him. He is in control. Once I decided to put God in control of my budget, it was like a 250-pound barbell being lightened to 100 pounds. The lift is much easier. My surrender to God's commands made it easier to find ways to simplify my life. By simplifying, I was able to redirect spending to support the Church's mission. I was beginning to do what I believed I was supposed to be doing. And it felt good. I worried less. I had less stress over our spending plan. That is my blessing. Thank you, Lord.

It is easy for me to say "Don't worry." In spite of serious medical expenses to deal with on top of fair amounts of support going to family and church, in truth, I suffered no actual financial strain. At least not any that wasn't of my own doing, such as a couple of real estate investments made right before the '08 market crash. Still, I really had nothing to worry about. But not worrying is hard to do. Now, it is easy to dispense platitudes and Bible verses, but hard not to worry when facing real-life challenges like losing a job, managing out-of-control debt, or facing exorbitant medical bills with no insurance. How are we not to worry when confronted by an unwanted divorce or when a business fails?

My brother had just such a business experience. He borrowed money from friends and family to start a business in a field he'd worked in for almost 20 years. He had a solid business plan and a supportive market. While not a sure thing, it seemed a good bet. Then it went south. He lost everything. For the next three years, he trudged along as a self-employed consultant. In other words, he had no income. He was out of cash and on the verge of bankruptcy.

But you know what? His family never missed a meal. It was often gumbo with a very thin roux, but they had something. How? He'd tell you that it was by the grace of God. People provided food and clothing. Sometimes an envelope with cash would be in the mailbox. He'd barter with merchants. He never lost faith. He was always in church and always put something in the basket. His relationship with the church community and with God was hugely important to him. Oh, he'd question God about the lessons God was trying to teach him, but he never doubted that things would work out for the good if he trusted. So, he trusted. Day-by-day. One day at a time. He saw no need to borrow trouble from the future. He focused on what God had for him and his family that day, and he trusted God would provide.

Miss Mary lost everything in Hurricane Katrina. She boarded a plane headed to a destination she did not know. Landing in Greenville, SC, a cot in an exhibition hall-turned-refugee-center became her home.

The community of St. Anthony Catholic Church adopted her. She shared this with me just the other day, "I lost everything, but look at how God has provided for me. I am so blessed. Fr. Pat was saying the other day that if anyone says they're happy all the time, they're lying. I disagree. I'm happy all the time."

"I was sitting out back yesterday and watching the leaves in the breeze and thought, How awesome is God? I thank God all day, every day. I say little prayers all day long. We can all find joy—even in the junk. If some mean thought sneaks into my brain, I get it out in two seconds. Ain't nothing gonna steal my joy.

"If someone needs something, I help them if I can, if it doesn't hurt me. No, wait a minute. I help them even if it does hurt me because I have so many friends here at church and in the neighborhood. I never need for nothing. I help people and people give to me. All I can say is, 'Thank you, God.'"

A church buddy shared his Stewardship story with me recently. In his own words,

"I was raised Catholic. In my adult years I drifted away from the church because of personal issues that I had (job loss, bankruptcy, and divorce). In the last couple of years, I started going to Gospel on Tap. When I told the men at my table that I was looking for a new place to call home and worship, one of them invited me to his church. I went, but didn't like it too much and realized that I needed my Catholicism back. I attended Mass on Ash Wednesday of this past year. I decided right then and there that I had found my home.

"A good thing happened on the following Sunday. Father announced the start of a 6:30 p.m. Mass and asked that people come and help out. So, I did. At the announcements, he said, 'Wouldn't it be nice if we had dinner after Mass?' I said to myself, Hey, I can cook. And the more I thought about it, the more I thought this could work. I really should say that the more I thought about it, the more the Holy Spirit moved me to make it work.

"I have to tell you that without a doubt, this has been the most worthwhile thing I have ever done. I'm putting my time and talent toward feeding the congregation, and I am more than happy to do it every week. Father mentioned once that I was slaving over a hot stove, but it's not that. This is my joy. It's not work at all. I admit that when it gets to crunch time, I get a bit nervous. But then I realize it's all going to work out and that I needn't worry. I had no clue how much to cook. God did, though, and He guided me!

"I was reading through the (Stewardship booklet) and I do spend a bit of my Time devoting my Talent to this endeavor. I estimate it's about 8 hours a week between the shopping and the cooking at church and at home. I do EFT for contributions and will probably up that from where I am right now. And my deal with Father is that if the money I spend for all the stuff needed for the meals is more than the donations I receive, I consider that to be my gift to the church. And if the donations I receive are more than my outlay, I give that excess to the school. A few weeks ago, I was able to donate $300.

"After a really difficult year, I feel that I am truly blessed and I believe that it is because I'm back to being at church, I'm back to being Catholic."

We are blessed, are we not?

We know it is more blessed to give than to receive (Acts 20:35). Think about your giving. When you give presents to loved ones, how do you feel? You probably put a lot of thought into what kind of present would be appreciated and enjoyed. You likely search diligently to find just the right gift that would delight the recipient. You watch with great anticipation as the gift is unwrapped and then beam with joy and delight as you are thanked. How wonderful the feeling when we give to those we love.

How is it with your gifts to the Lord? Where does God rank in your list of loved ones? Are you as diligent and intentional with your gifts to Him? Attitude is important. Giving to the Lord out of love is the gift He longs for, like rain in the desert. If instead, giving comes from a sense of obligation, then it is just charity: "If I give away everything I own…but do not have love, I gain nothing" (1 Cor. 13:3). When giving is "as a contribution to the Lord" (Num. 18:24), then it becomes an act of worship. Giving deepens our faith. We give to what and who we love.

STEWARDSHIP REFLECTION

Who and what do you love?

Like the rich man in Mark 10, we must decide who Jesus is and where He ranks in our lives. We also must face the truth about where we rank our possessions. Are they equally as important to us as our relationship with Jesus?

If they are, doesn't that impair and cloud our relationship with God? Are we willing to follow Jesus' advice to sell our possessions to rid ourselves of unhealthy attachments that distance us from deepening our relationship with God, deepening our trust in God?

Decide who and what you love best. Choose God and detach from everything else. Detach and give. Give because It's Not Your Money.

Elizabeth lives a stewardship witness as profound as any I've ever encountered. She is always at church—she attends Sunday Mass, of course, and many weekday Masses, sings in two choirs, attends Adult Education programs, volunteers for many ministries, and gives at the level of a tithe, if not more. I complimented and thanked her for the wonderful support she gives to the church, and asked her why she did it. She told me that after some very difficult circumstances in her early 30s, she realized how blessed she was and rededicated her life to Christ and His church.

Those circumstances revolved around an abusive marriage to an alcoholic. Over a cup of coffee she told me, "I saw evidence of alcoholism before the wedding, but went ahead with it anyway. I did not see the signs of the abuse to come. Still, I tried to work through it. We went to counseling, but nothing changed."

Elizabeth went on to tell me how they married in the Church against the advice of her parents and her pastor. "He had a hard time holding a job for very long, but I work as a physician and so made decent money. He just assumed we could afford the so-called good life. It may have even appeared to others that we did. But he often spent so much on booze and carousing that we had to scramble to pay the utilities." She mentioned how in hindsight, she feels she ignored Christ. She thought that as a smart and accomplished professional, she could handle it on her own. She finally got a divorce.

"I couldn't believe the hell I was living. The abuse got worse. I had to get out. I didn't ask God 'Why?' I knew why. After my divorce, I dedicated myself to God and my daughter. I simplified my life. I live modestly." After a sip of coffee, she went on to say, "You know, my life hasn't turned out the way I dreamed of when I was a little girl. But I am so blessed. And I am deeply grateful for God's faithfulness. He brought me back to the Church and this community. What a privilege to be a member here and participate in all the good that goes on here. I am so thankful for the ways God allows me to give. I wish I could give more."

The personal stories above give witness that clearly, we can trust God. If we believe what He says, if we only have faith as small as a mustard seed, we can trust Him. When we reflect on the astounding truth that the Creator of the universe is smitten with each of us individually and the astonishing news of Jesus' suffering and death for each of us, His phenomenal resurrection then gives us faith and hope that we have an inheritance that is imperishable (Peter 1:3-4). How then can we have any sense of pride or arrogance about anything we may have accomplished or acquired? How can we have any doubt or fear about the future? How can we be anything but humble and grateful and generous?

C. S. Lewis in *Mere Christianity* posits, "One of the dangers of having a lot of money is that you may be quite satisfied with the kind of happiness money can give, and so fail to realize your need for God… you may forget that you are at every moment totally dependent on God."[30] He states this paradox: "The only things we can keep are the things we freely give to God. What we try to keep for ourselves is just what we are sure to lose."[31]

What is it that we try to keep for ourselves? To what do we cling? In John 20:17 as Jesus was preparing to ascend to the Father, Mary Magdalene clung to Him, trying to keep Him from going. He had to tell her to let go so that He could ascend to the Father and send the Holy Spirit for the good of all of us. When Paul left Ephesus after spending three years there, the people clung to him. They didn't want him to leave them (Acts 20:37). What do we need to let go of so that we can become holy? What is in the way of our giving and realizing the riches of our inheritance in Christ?

STEWARDSHIP REFLECTION

Detach

How many people do we see in our society who have exceeding talent and tremendous success and wealth, and yet they're not happy? Like the rich man in Matthew 19 who had many possessions, they know something is missing in their lives.

Even people who consider themselves to be ordinary middle-class have a kind of angst driven by the urge for more. More what? We don't know, but we know something is missing. Maybe we can purchase just what we need.

Instead, Jesus tells us to detach ourselves from earthly possessions, detach from desire for stuff. Things don't bring us true happiness. They're often the leading cause of increased stress and worry in our lives.

What are you attached to? Attachment to anything other than God is idolatry. Get rid of it! Sell it. Give to the poor. Trust God. Follow Jesus. And give gladly because It's Not Your Money.

God loves us radically, unreservedly. We can't help but love in return when we are so loved. To love is to give. God gives extravagantly, lavishly. We can't help but give in return. But we are hesitant to give money. Money seems to have a mesmerizing power over us. We stubbornly believe we need more of it or we're deathly afraid we won't have enough of it. Can we hand over to God the power money has over our lives? Pope Benedict XVI says, "The only way to liberation is the complete dependence on love, which would then also be true freedom." As God is love, total dependence and trust in Him and obedience to His Word is true freedom, true peace.

We have hopes and dreams for our future. But how often do we think about, much less emphasize, our eternal future? If you are like me, waiting for a future benefit is not in my nature. Patience is a challenge. I want what I want and I want it now. When I don't get it, even after fervent prayer in all good intention, it cracks open the door to hurtful pride and stokes the fire of doubt and fear. The drive for and expectation of immediate gratification is the by-product of our consumer society.

This is not God's way. We need to nurture an eternal perspective. We should be more concerned about storing up treasure in heaven. Jesus tell us in Mt. 6:19-21 not to store up treasure on earth, but to store it in heaven so that our hearts will be there in heaven with Him. How do we do that? By giving Him our hearts. That is what He really wants. When He has our hearts, we will want to give Him our Time, Talent, and Treasure. Returning these gifts to the Lord is one way we "seek first the kingdom of God, and His righteousness, and all these things will be given you besides" (Mt. 6: 33). Giving these gifts is one way we demonstrate a mature discipleship.

Paul tells us in Phil. 3:20 that we are citizens of heaven, and Peter urges in 1 Pet. 2:11 that as sojourners, we are to keep away from worldly desires that wage war against the soul. Hence, everything we say and do should be geared toward our future home. C. S. Lewis calls hope our focus on the future. Our aim, our goal and objective, should be Heaven, he says: "Aim at Heaven and you will get earth thrown in."[32]

Is all this just "religie" cliché? Do you really think of yourself as a citizen of heaven? Do you truly believe God will provide? You've read real-life stories of that provision in this book. You've probably experienced it yourself. So why hesitate to trust and give? The Lord is good to those who trust Him. His acts of mercy are inexhaustible. His compassion is never depleted. They are renewed each morning (Lam. 3:22-25). We are to have no anxiety, but to submit everything to God—even our financial needs and concerns (Phil. 4:6).

As I said earlier, my favorite stewardship Bible passage is Malachi 3:7-10. God at once admonishes us, but then challenges us.

He almost taunts us:

God: "(Make a) return to me, that I may return to you."

Us: "Why should we (make a) return to you?"

God: "Can anyone rob God? Yet, you are robbing me."

Us: "How have we robbed you?"

God: "In tithes and in offerings. Bring the whole tithe into the store-house. Put me to the test, and see if I won't open the floodgates of heaven for you and pour down upon you blessings without measure."

Try Him in this. Put Him to the test. Trust and give—not with a give-to-get, "prosperity gospel" attitude, but in love and gratefulness for all the blessings and benefits God gives to you—and then see if, in this action, you begin to feel a sense of peace that comes from being obedient to His Word.

We pray for peace at Mass in the Eucharistic celebration. We ask our merciful Father in humble prayer and petition through Jesus Christ to be pleased to grant us peace. In the Lord's prayer we ask Him to deliver us from every evil and graciously grant us peace in our days. At the Sign of Peace, Jesus tell us, "Peace I leave you, my peace I give to you…and grant (us) peace in unity." In this peace, our trust and faith will grow stronger. We will want to give more. We will gain even greater peace and joy.

Once we know and believe how truly blessed we are, we will let go of whatever it is we cling to and whatever it is that we're afraid of. We will trust that God will provide. We will take that step of faith and give. And we will experience God's love and care for us as He opens the floodgates of heaven and pours out blessings upon blessings. We will then know His peace, a peace which surpasses all understanding (Phil. 4:7). That is what this book is about—finding peace. Peace with ourselves. Peace in our households. Peace with our neighbors. Peace throughout the world.

I hope you read in this book the Bible's message of how to align your finances and your life with God's way. It is the only true path to peace and joy. Isn't that what we want? God has given each of us a spirit of wisdom and revelation that we may know the riches of glory in His inheritance (Eph. 1:17-18). Believing this, we are transformed. We love more. We give more. More works of mercy are performed. That is attractive to others. We become beacons of light in the world. Others are brought closer to God through us. They, too, will want that sense of peace, that spirit of God in us. Then together, as dedicated, intentional stewards of all the gifts God gives to us, we will transform our communities and our Church. We will change the world. What a legacy to build and leave to our loved ones! We will make heaven here on earth.

Be well!

FRUIT OF THE SPIRIT

FORTITUDE
*The moral virtue that ensures firmness in difficulties
and constancy in the pursuit of the good.
It strengthens the resolve to resist temptations, to overcome obstacles,
and to conquer fear.*

Examples: **ST. IGNATIUS and ST. FRANCIS**
Both of whom renounced vast wealth and founded orders which have transformed the practice of our faith.

Mt. 21:21
"If you have faith and do not waver...you (can) say to this mountain, 'Be lifted up and thrown into the sea,' and it will be done."

Peace Beyond Understanding

"Make extravagant generosity your greatest vice
and become God-like."

Fr. Edward Hays

ACKNOWLEDGMENTS

Always first and foremost, all thanks, praise, honor, and glory to God for all the blessings and benefits he gives to me. Thank you to my family for all their love and support through the years. And a special thank you to Claire, my fiancé, who has had to learn to put up with the time demands and stresses of writing, rewriting, publishing, and marketing a book.

This book wouldn't be what it is without the courageous criticisms of Bob Lange, Bill Wrenn, and Michael Brennan. Also, the encouragement of Brian Pusateri, Mike and Mark Thompson, Joe Valitchka, and all my Cursillo brothers helped me persevere, as did the feedback from Mike Giordano and Zach Gilliam. Chuck Milteer and Loraine Angel provided keen editing for which I am grateful. Chris Pelicano's talents in design made the presentation of the message much more readable. To all of you—thank you.

A special shout-out goes to J. T. Curtis and all the Curtis family. Their love and leadership in my young life was so important to my formation as a Christian and as a man. I owe a debt of gratitude to them that words are inadequate to express.

I am honored by my association with Jon and Evelyn Bean, cofounders of Compass Catholic Ministries. I look forward to what the Holy Spirit will do with this book in partnership with their ministry in service to God's kingdom.

And to Fr. Patrick Tuttle—my pastor. I remember our meeting in January 2017 when he offered an opportunity for me to join the parish staff as Director of Stewardship. We both were surprised and nervous about our ability to work together. But by the grace of God, we recognized the promptings of the Holy Spirit and thankfully, said "Yes." Fr. Pat's gentle, patient, and loving guidance has been pivotal in my gaining a much fuller understanding of stewardship. You, dear reader, are the beneficiary.

It's Not Your Money

ENDNOTES

INTRODUCTION

1. Brian Starks and Christian Smith, University of Notre Dame Institute for Church Life, *Unleashing Catholic Generosity* (2012), 4

2. Charles Zech and Michael Castrilli, Villanova University Center for Church Management

CHAPTER ONE

CHAPTER TWO

3. Ken Blanchard and Associates, *Leading at a Higher Level* (Upper Saddle, NJ: Prentice Hall, 2007) pp 259-260

4. Francis, *Gaudete et Exultate* (2018), 10

5. Robert Barron. *Letter to a Suffering Church* (2019), 92

6. E Christian Brugger. National Catholic Register, *How Can I Discern God's Will?* April 19, 2018 (*Novo Millennio Inuente*, 31)

7. Francis, *Gaudete et Exsultate*, 23 and 21

8. US Conference of Catholic Bishops, *Stewardship: A Disciple's Response* (1983) 1, 4, and 8

9. Paul J. Achtemeier, *Harper Collins Bible Dictionary* (Harper San Francisco, 1996), 443

10. Walter Bruggeman, *Money and Possessions* (Westminster John Knox Press, 2016), xix

11. Ibid., xx

12. Ibid., 185-203

13. CCC 1832

14. Brueggeman, *Money and Possessions*, 11

15. Ken passed away 7 weeks after our conversation.

16. GK Chesteron, *Orthodoxy* (Image Books, 1959), 65

17. Cindy Wooden, Catholic News Service, Pope speaks of holiness as being loving, full of life, The Catholic Miscellany, April 12, 2018

18. USCCB, *Stewardship, a Disciples Response*, 13

19. Ibid., 4 and 47

20. Matthew Kelly, *The Four Signs of a Dynamic Catholic* (Beacon Publishing 2012), 12-14

21. Charles E. Zech, "The Ten Essential Building Blocks to Developing a Stewardship Parish", in Paul A. Holmes (ed) *A Pastor's Toolbox 2: More Management Skills for Parish Leadership* (Collegeville: Liturgical Press, 2017), pp 79-90

22. Achtemeier, *Harper Collins Bible Dictionary*, 174-175 and 625

23. Dave Sutherland and Kirk Nowery, *The 33 Laws of Stewardship* (NewSource Publishing 2003), 89

24. Achtemeier, *Harper Collins Bible Dictionary*, 326 and 328

CHAPTER THREE

25. Howard Dayton and Jon and Evelyn Bean, *Your Money Counts,* Chapter 14 (Compass Catholic Ministries 2011)

26. Achtemeier, *Harper Collins Bible Dictionary*, 1214

27. Brueggeman, *Money and Possessions*, 5

28. Kelly, dynamiccatholic.com

29. Dayton, *Your Money Counts*, 116

CHAPTER FOUR

30. CS Lewis, *Mere Christianity* (MacMillan Publishing Co., 1952), 180

31. Ibid 180
32. Ibid 118

NOTES

NOTES

_____

_____

_____

_____

_____

_____

_____

_____

_____

_____

_____

_____

_____

_____

_____

_____

_____

_____

_____

_____

NOTES

NOTES

_____

_____

_____

_____

_____

_____

_____

_____

_____

_____

_____

_____

_____

_____

_____

_____

_____

NOTES

_____
_____
_____
_____
_____
_____
_____
_____
_____
_____
_____
_____
_____
_____
_____
_____
_____
_____
_____
_____